Ambassadors to Muslims

Building Bridges to the Gospel

Fouad Masri

AMBASSADORS TO MUSLIMS: BUILDING BRIDGES TO THE GOSPEL

ISBN-13: 978-098475-490-8

Cover and interior design by Niddy Griddy Design, Inc.

Cover photo: © iStock Photo

LCCN: 2011941390

Printed in the United States of America

2 3 4 5 6 7 8 / 16 15 14 13

to Karen,
Thank you for showing the Hope!

[illegible]
Eph. 2:10
Jn 3:16

Dedication

This book is dedicated to my best friend and wife, Lisa,
and my two precious children.

Acknowledgments

It is by God's grace that we finished this book. He provided the assistance of the following people, whom I also thank: my parents, Adel and Doha Masri; my wife, Lisa, and my children; Brian Smith, my editor; Betsy Gutwin and the rest of the staff and volunteers of Crescent Project; and Karen Pickering and Tom Addington of Book Villages.

Contents

Introduction

The dream of students worldwide had come true for me: the chance to study in the United States of America. The prospect of earning a degree in "the land of opportunity" would have been a thrill for any eighteen-year-old Lebanese boy.

It was 1980 when I flew from Beirut to JFK Airport in New York City. It was my first visit to the United States. I filled my flying time meeting lots of new people and watching American movies. I also spent time reading *The Greatest Collection of Clean American Jokes*, a book someone had given me before I left Beirut—my first attempt at understanding the American sense of humor. Some of the jokes were funny, but most of them I found boring. Admittedly, I never quite understood the punch lines.

When I stepped into the JFK Airport, I tried to draw upon my past experience to make sense of my surroundings. I had been told that America was a Christian nation, and in Lebanon a person's religion is clearly evident from his dress or name. But here before my eyes, I saw no evidence of a standard of attire, by which to tell a person's religion. Who were the Christians? Who were not? Some wore colorful dresses, others wore crisp business suits. I was totally confused.

I was also shocked by the diversity of nationalities. It's not that I expected to be surrounded by Arabs, as had been true in Lebanon. But I suppose I expected some type of uniformity. The whole world seemed to have converged on the place! Not just Latinos or Caucasians or Asians or Africans, but a thorough mix of all.

The airport was only the first of many mental challenges for me. My first school was a liberal arts college in the Midwest, and it wasn't long before my name became an issue on campus. The American students found "Fouad" difficult to pronounce. They just couldn't say it. One student on my floor actually called me "Food" for a whole semester. (In spite of the difficulty for some, I'm still proud of my given name, which in Arabic means "loving heart." For the record, you can pronounce it "Fwad," like "quad," but with an *F*.)

My knowledge of American slang was tested when my classmate's brother started a new job. I asked how the job was going, and he told me, "They already gave him the boot."

Inwardly I wondered why his brother had been given a cowboy's footwear. I probed further: "Why did they do that?"

My classmate responded, "Well, you know, my brother was low on the totem pole."

I had learned English, but not *that* kind of English.

Muslims in Montana

In 1981 I began traveling in the Midwest and across the United States, and I quickly became aware of the growing Muslim population all across North America. I'd find Muslims in the strangest places. Sudanese Muslims in farming communities. A mosque near Walla Walla, Washington. A *halal* store in Garden Grove, California.

When I met some of these people, I discovered that many of their struggles were identical to mine: learning English, making sense of this culture without religious cues, and understanding the Western mindset.

I met a Moroccan student named Tariq at the University of Illinois, who drove two hours just to hang out with me and some other Arab students because he had no friends at his school. He asked if I understood Americans, explaining, "I like Americans, but I do not understand them."

"What don't you understand about them?" I asked.

"They always say, 'See you later,' but I never see them again." Tariq misunderstood American slang, and so he considered Americans undependable and inauthentic.

Many of the Muslims I met were also grappling with spiritual questions. I began my graduate work in Islamic studies at Fuller Theological Seminary in Pasadena, California, and I became more aware of the great spiritual need that existed among Muslims all over North America. Even though Muslims were living in "the land of the free," most of them still had never read a page of the New Testament. They were not being invited to Christian homes, and very few had heard a clear presentation about who Jesus is and why He came. On the whole, the Muslims I met were lonely, out of touch with the surrounding society, and spiritually famished. What could be done?

Sharing the Hope with Muslims

After serving in Lebanon for ten years, in 1992 I proposed to a wonderful lady named Lisa (under the beautiful cedars of Lebanon), and we were married later that same year. She shared my urgent concern for the spiritual state of Muslims in North America, and together we formed Crescent Project in 1993. We knew we were called by God to share the hope of Christ with Muslims. The ministry's beginnings were modest. We had two hundred dollars in a bank account, and our home office was meagerly furnished with a desk and a monstrous Apple word processor. But our ministry vision was God-sized.

We soon realized that our mission couldn't just be directly to Muslims, but also indirectly by motivating and mobilizing more Christians to get involved. We needed to multiply our efforts, and we were convinced that impacting Muslims with the gospel wasn't rocket science. With proper training, using simple, practical steps, any of Christ's followers could share the good news of Jesus with a Muslim.

Then came the obstacles—not opposition, but apathy. Most churches we approached seemed unconcerned about the growing population of lost and searching Muslims around them. Church people didn't want to deal with Islam, so they lived in denial. One pastor said to me, "There are no Muslims in my city"; he lived five minutes from the largest mosque in his state. Some Christians I met were paralyzed by fear of the unknown. Others had good intentions, but they didn't know where to start.

We learned two things: first, that we did not have the power to light a fire under Christians; second, that God did. I saw God at work in the heart of a young campus ministry worker named Josh. Josh enjoyed interacting with college students, but he intentionally avoided the Muslims on campus. Why? He didn't know how to share with them and didn't want to get in over his head. I spent two hours with him in a one-on-one training session, laying out how to share his faith with Muslims, and he walked away visibly more confident and full of faith that God could use him to reach Muslims.

One week later I got a phone call from Josh. "Please pray for me today, Fouad. I've invited a student from Pakistan to have coffee with me. Pray that I can share about Jesus." Josh had a great conversation with Muhammad, who ended up requesting a copy of the New Testament. The relationship continued and grew throughout Josh's time in school.

After hearing numerous such stories, I have become convinced that God is willing to enable any of His followers to confidently bear witness about Jesus to Muslims.

September 11: A Wake-Up Call

Jesus had been stirring in the heart of the American church for years, but in September 2001, America was more than stirred—we were shaken. When it came to Muslims, attitudes and interest levels changed in a matter of hours. Talk shows discussed Muslim religious beliefs and practices. American women watched news clips of burqa-clad women in Afghanistan, barred from schools and jobs and relegated to their homes. A sweet elderly lady came to me, concern on her face, and asked me, "Have they always lived that way?"

And our ministry changed overnight. Before, I spent my days knocking on pastors' office doors, trying to get an appointment, hoping to explain the need to reach Muslims. Now the same pastors were knocking on *my* door. Every weekend I spoke in a different church, attempting to explain the difficult issues surrounding September 11. Whole congregations dealt with anger, sorrow, and deep concern over the attacks, and we did our best to answer questions like: "Why do they hate us?" "Are all Muslims terrorists?" and "How should we live in light of September 11?"

The events of September 11 were tragic, yet I continue to see how God turned what was intended for evil and used it for good in His kingdom. The church needed to be jolted awake to an awareness of Muslims' presence and need for the gospel. Just as Jesus endured the cross, looking to the reward of His suffering, I believe the suffering of that day has borne fruit for the gospel that outweighs the intended evil.

Why I Wrote This Book

The world of Islam still mystifies Christians. Nearly every day we hear of another car bombing. Internet headlines relentlessly remind us of problems in the Middle East. We can't escape the messages, but do we understand what they mean? Do we read these headlines in light of the gospel? Until the church views Muslims through the eyes of Jesus Christ, rather than those of the news media, the followers of Jesus will not impact the Muslim world.

I wrote this book in order to inform and equip you, the reader, to play a role in Christ's harvest among Muslims. In the early chapters, we will delve into the basics about Islam and the Quran, to help you understand Muslims, what they believe, and how they view the world. Next, this book will give you simple, practical steps for reaching out—including pointers for opening spiritual conversations and answering tough questions. Along the way, I'll share from my own and others' personal experiences of the Lord of the harvest at work, revealing Himself to Muslim students, professionals, refugees, and converts, changing their lives for eternity.

God is moving among Muslims—perhaps even in your community. I desire that *Ambassadors to Muslims* would help you grow in love toward these neighbors and in confidence that Jesus Christ can and will use you to guide Muslims into His kingdom of light.

Chapter One

Because I Hate

"The thief comes only to steal and kill and destroy; I have come that they may have life, and have it to the full."
—Jesus in John 10:10

On a clear Tuesday morning, I made my way to a missions committee meeting, praising God for His wonderful creation. I walked into the church and greeted the pastors and committee. I was about to launch into my presentation when a receptionist stuck her head in the door. "Excuse me, but you'll want to see what's going on. There's an attack on New York City."

You probably remember where you were on the morning of September 11, 2001. This generation's equivalent of Pearl Harbor left every American shocked and shaken. The images played and replayed on the news are emblazoned on our minds: the first World Trade Center tower burning and collapsing, the second plane careening into the other tower as the world gasped and gaped. My missions committee presentation didn't happen. Instead we prayed together and wept for the sin that led to such theft of life.

The Thief in the Middle East

Look at the Middle East, and you'll see that the "thief" of which Jesus spoke is alive and well, stealing, killing, and destroying in the region. The news is filled with Israelis fighting Palestinians, Kurds hating Turks, or

Shi'ites ostracized by Sunnis. The Syrians are occupying Lebanon, while the Iraqis are threatened by Iran. The murderous thief is active in the Middle East.

This is the environment into which I was born. In Beirut, Lebanon, I grew up hating both Palestinians and Israelis. My solution for the crisis in the Middle East would have been to take both sides to a desert, let them fight, and whoever wins, give them the dusty piece of land. Be done with it!

My hatred didn't emerge overnight. It grew gradually, starting at an early age. When I was six, I helped my father tape paper to the windows inside our apartment. The brown paper, torn from a roll and taped against the glass, would keep light from escaping through our windows. By blacking out our building, we and our neighbors hoped to avoid becoming a target of the Israeli jets and bombs that riddled our city.

It was June 1967, and the Six-Day War had begun between the state of Israel and several Arab nations. Although my parents showed us love and tried to shield us from the violence, the turmoil of our community unavoidably broke through to our young ears and eyes.

The Italians' Fault

As I headed into my teen years, I heard daily anti-Semitic statements and slurs. A

CULTURAL POINTER

Interact men with men, women with women. Men and women are usually separated in Islam, and piety and purity respected (as they are in Christianity). Women, always dress modestly and do not enter a gathering of all men. Men, do not enter a home where no other men are present.

IN ACTION

Help the traumatized and displaced. Today, more than ever, the Muslim world is going through change and political upheaval. Many Muslims are refugees who have experienced or witnessed violence. You can provide a listening ear, help with practical needs, and share with them about their greatest friend, Jesus the Messiah.

common phrase was *Al-haq ala al-tilyan*—"It is the Italians' fault." The Italians' fault? For what? When Italy joined the Allies in World War II, it led to the fall of Hitler and the Third Reich, halting the total eradication of the Jewish people. When my neighbors and acquaintances were frustrated with the political situation, they would blame the mess on the Italians' failure to help do away with Jews.

Also heard often on the streets of Beirut was a rhyme chanted by Palestinian mobs, marching to decry political decisions. The chant went, *Khaybar, Khaybar ya Yahoud, saif Muhammad la yamout*. Khaybar is the historical city where one of Muhammad's battles took place. There, his army overthrew a Jewish settlement and eventually killed the inhabitants. Literally translated, the song was a chilling threat: "Jews everywhere, remember Khaybar! For the sword of Muhammad will never die or rest."

Life in Lebanon was charged with wars, urban battles and new militias forming everywhere. Each group rose up claiming to be bringers of lasting peace. The problems? They were blamed on someone else. Another race, another religion, another politician, another government.

My mother was Syrian, but I was born and raised in my father's native Lebanon, so I grew up proudly Lebanese. The Lebanese are known for their unflinching nationalism.

CULTURAL POINTER

Be sensitive to your friend's responses. If he or she seems unwilling to answer a question you have posed, maybe it is too invasive a question for this stage in the relationship. Simply move on or share a story of your own.

But when I saw Lebanese militias fighting and killing fellow countrymen—Sunnis on Christians on Shi'ites—my patriotism waned. And when I saw mercenaries from other countries fighting on Lebanese soil—my soil, my neighborhood—my heart grew cold. *This is my neighborhood*, I thought. *Where my grandmother lives, where my cousins and I go to school. Go back to your country and leave us alone.*

Throughout my teen years the deaths of friends and neighbors at the hands of Israelis and Palestinians caused me to harbor deep hatred for both. I had never met an Israeli—or any Jewish person—yet I hated them and wished them ill. When F-4 Phantom jets swooped over Lebanon, I cursed the Israeli men and women who manned them and secretly wished them destroyed.

The Seed of Hate

April 13, 1975, was another sunny day in Beirut. I had just returned home from school when we turned on the radio and heard about the most recent violence. In East Beirut, a shootout between a bus filled with Palestinians and residents of a Christian-majority neighborhood had left several dead and wounded.

Although my family lived in a different part of town, the events of the day jarred me. That night I lay awake, listening to the mortar shells exploding in other districts.

Machine guns and bazookas fired. Rocket-propelled grenades blasted for hours on end. The Lebanese Civil War had begun, and slowly all of West Beirut came under the control of the PLO (Palestinian Liberation Organization). My life was heading into what would be a long, dark tunnel. For the first few days, I was excited that school was cancelled, even though the reason was grim. But as the war wore on, I was hit with the reality that school could be cancelled indefinitely. Would I ever graduate and go to college? Any thoughts I had for my future were up in the air, out of my control.

My parents tried to instill hope in our family. One evening, not long after the war had begun, my brothers, my sister, and I sat together in silence, listening to the bombs explode in the distance. My father, Adel, walked over to the cabinet, removed his violin, and started playing. His renditions of traditional tunes and old hymns gradually overcame the sound of mortar shelling. In time, our family began to laugh and sing along. The evening ended with a competitive game of Risk.

Those moments were the lights in my tunnel's otherwise pervasive darkness. Violence escalated and PLO fighters were more and more common in our neighborhood. Wherever you went, there were checkpoints. No place was sacred or off limits in the militias' eyes. The Lebanese War, fought primarily in urban, residential quarters, targeted tourist areas, hotel districts, and outer suburbs. Militants fought in churches and mosques, burning religious symbols and murdering religious leaders. Human life was worth nothing. Fighters showed no respect for children, women, or unarmed civilians. People were killed because they were from the wrong religion in the wrong part of town.

The militias adopted religious-sounding names like "Christian Militia" and "Hezbollah" (meaning "the party of God"), claiming God's backing and blessing on their killing. Each militia felt justified—the Druze against the Maronite Catholics, Shi'ites versus Sunnis, the Sunnis against the Maronites, and on and on.

On a Saturday morning, around nine a.m., my friend Waleed was walking down the street on his way to the corner market. Waleed and I played soccer together in school, and he had been a good friend to me. He turned the corner just as a mortar shell landed and exploded, killing him instantly. My good friend Waleed was eighteen years old.

Deadly Harvest

Sin in all its flagrant rawness was always in our faces. In the West, I've found that sin comes wearing a suit and a tie and goes by the name of "scandal." But in the Middle East, sin is explicit, shameless—garishly raw. For about a year, our city saw one car bomb per week. I don't have words to describe the sickening anxiety I felt when walking past a row of cars. *Am I passing a time bomb? Is it that Mercedes ahead? Is it that Pinto over there? Which car will go off next?*

It was during these dark days that a group of ruthless fighters emerged, called *al-Qanaseen*—the Snipers. Their purpose was to pick off civilians associated with the opposing side. They would sit on a rooftop or in an apartment building window and target any defenseless person crossing the street below. One unforgettable event involving *al-Qanaseen* struck the crippling blow to my already weakening faith, causing it to crumble. I saw the replay on TV: A young woman holding her child was timidly crossing a downtown street. A sniper, waiting in the top floor of a nearby building, shot her in the knee. She crumpled to the ground in the middle of the intersection, screaming. Next, the sniper shot the small child in the head. Then, after the woman had watched her baby die, he finished by shooting and killing the mother.

The public watched in helpless shock and grief. For me, the event was paramount. It made me completely doubt the existence of God. *Where is He? Why doesn't He stop these things? If God is really there, how can He simply watch while this war rages on? Why would a good God allow such blatant, blasphemous wrong, such raw evil?*

After watching the barbaric murder of that innocent woman and her child, I chose to become a practical atheist. I figured the existence or nonexistence of God had no bearing on the mess that was my home, my country. But my time as an atheist was short; God cannot be examined under a microscope and proven to not exist. So I concluded that agnosticism was for me. I didn't know what to believe, and this label sounded intellectual. My latest form of arrogance lasted a few weeks, until I opted for deism—that is, belief in a powerful Creator who has become disinterested in humankind. I felt this best explained my state of affairs and this ridiculous war.

I continued to toy with different teachings and philosophies. But no matter how far afield I ventured, I was continually haunted by Christ's outrageous claims. He said that when you hate your brother, it is the same as killing him. At first that statement did not make sense to me, but as I further investigated the history of the Lebanese War—not to mention my own life experience—I realized it had started with brothers and neighbors hating one another. Hatred passed along from one generation to the next, instilled in impressionable children's minds, later resulted in killing and war. This war had not started in April 13, 1975, but in earlier eras when people from different religious groups and nationalities began to harbor hatred toward one other. Killing is the harvest we reap from the seed called hate.

Killing is the harvest we reap from the seed called hate.

Christ's words kept echoing in my mind. If what He said was true—and deep down I knew it was—that meant that the hate I felt toward Palestinians and Israelis made me no better than any other killer. In God's eyes I wasn't just a sinner; I was a murderer.

In God's eyes I wasn't just a sinner; I was a murderer.

Tipping Point

About this time, the war's evil struck a family that were friends of ours. They were having dinner when their two-year-old son spilled his drink all over himself. The father had just taken him to the bathroom to wash him up when a mortar shell sailed through the balcony door and exploded in the middle of the family's table, killing the mother and other children. Only the father and his young son survived. The man buried his family that week.

This was the tipping point in my spiritual journey. Even as a young man, I could see that the problem in the Middle East was not weapons or politics. The real problem stemmed from a heart condition—hatred. And I was a hater.

I went to my room and closed the door. I knelt beside my bed and prayed this prayer: "Lord Jesus, You healed the sick, raised the dead, and forgave Your enemies. Forgive me for my sin of hate, and change my heart and mind. The more war I see in Lebanon, the more I want to be a soldier of Your peace. The more hatred I see in Lebanon, the more I want to be a soldier of love."

With this simple prayer of repentance and dedication, God began a change in my heart. I saw evidence of this change about two weeks later when I met Nadim, a former classmate, on the campus of the American University of Beirut. Nadim was a Palestinian. I found that all my hatred and resentment for Nadim had been displaced by the compassion of Christ. I saw him as someone in need of the gospel.

Nadim and I had never spoken to one another, but that day I shared with him my faith in Christ and His teachings. I told him about my decision to follow Christ and to

IN ACTION

Always Share. Choose one of the ways you've experienced God's transforming power in your life. In private or with a Christian friend, practice telling the story in less than three minutes—the shorter the better. Then tell it to a Muslim friend.

extend His compassion to others around me. Nadim was surprised and interested, and he asked for a copy of the *Injeel*—the New Testament. I walked away from that encounter knowing that only Jesus Christ could have given me love for my neighbor—and for my enemy—Nadim.

New Eyes

Slowly, Christ was changing the way I viewed the world. As I prayed for Palestinians and Israelis, God took me into His operating room and performed an eye transplant. I no longer saw enemies, but souls in need of salvation. My church offered a small weekly prayer group, in which we prayed for national leaders from all sides, like Yasser Arafat, Saddam Hussein, Muammar al-Qaddafi, and Menachem Begin. As my friends and I interceded, God showed me that He is brokenhearted for every person, Christian or not. He desires that all might have life in abundance.

Five years later, I had become involved in Christian ministry and was regularly sharing my faith in Christ with others. I was invited to a Christian conference in Korea, and when I arrived at the conference center in Seoul, I looked at the name of my assigned roommate and balked. Apparently my spiritual maturity still left something to be desired. "Ilan" sounded Jewish—very Jewish. The conference organizers had placed an Israeli and an Arab in the same room. What were they thinking?

But Ilan was a Jewish believer in Christ. He called himself Messianic. Throughout the conference, I was surprised by his sincere faith and his diligence in following Christ and His teachings. Even more surprising, I found myself praying with him for our countries and responding to him with compassion. What more evidence did I need of Christ's complete one-eighty in my life? I was rooming with an Israeli and I bore him no ill feelings—only brotherly love.

When I asked Ilan about the Christian community and those he fellowships with in Israel, I expected him to describe a Messianic Jewish congregation. When he told me he worshipped with an Arab congregation, I was thrown off.

"Why?" I asked.

"Why not?" he responded. "They are my brothers and sisters in the faith."

Ilan's answer made all the pieces come together. It dawned on me that the solution to the ongoing Middle East crisis was forgiveness—a value shift from hate to love. Peace will come when Jesus Christ empowers a Palestinian to say to an Israeli, "I forgive you," and when an Israeli says to a Palestinian, "I forgive you." As long as Israelis raise their children to hate Palestinians, and vice versa, peace will never reign in the Middle East. Until forgiveness is possible, peace is unattainable. Sadly, the problem in the Middle East is not only political—it is mainly spiritual.

Until forgiveness is possible, peace is unattainable.

Five Boys and a Scrap of Paper

Although the aggression toward the United States came as a shock to most Americans, I had grown up knowing *jihad*. In 1983, when a suicide bomber rammed a van into the US Embassy in Beirut, I came across the scene mere minutes after the explosion. It was practically in my neighborhood. I watched in dismay as American Marines picked up the bodies of dead and wounded from the rubble. That same day an anonymous letter was sent to the press. It declared that "*jihad* has begun" against America.

I experienced being hated because I was a Christian. In fact, one classmate, named Kamal, told me plainly, "Once the *jihad* is declared, as a Muslim, it would be an honor for me to kill you."

Kamal was one of five classmates who, in their deep-seated hatred, wanted to kill an American before they died. Early in high school, I came across the five of them huddled around a desk, looking at a poorly-printed map of North America. Curious, I leaned over Kamal's shoulder to get a look at the crumpled scrap of paper. Ten dots were scribbled on the map, and one dot on the eastern coastline had these letters written carefully next to it—WTC.

"What is this, Kamal?" I asked.

"That's the World Trade Center," he explained. "It's this place in New York. We are going to hijack ten planes over the United States and crash them in these places." He moved his finger from dot to dot. "We want to punish Americans for what is happening here."

Fast forward once again to September 11, 2001. As I sat with the church missions committee, through tear-blurred eyes I watched the aftermath of the first plane's collision and actually saw the second plane strike its tower. When the news anchor announced that two other planes had been hijacked, you know what I was thinking. My mind was on Kamal and his ten planes that would "punish the Americans." Through the fog in my mind I remembered the words of Jesus in John 10:10: "The thief comes to kill, steal and destroy." (ESV) Only Satan could be behind such a massacre.

But the rest of the verse—the promise of Jesus—is what brings hope to those who trust in Jesus. He draws a sharp contrast between His purpose and the enemy's when He says, "I came that they may have life and have it abundantly." (ESV)

I Am the Problem: Jesus Is the Solution

This was the hope that I shared in response to the flurry of questions that came my way after September 11. In churches, in schools, on radio programs, while Americans grappled with a new, bewildering reality, I provided much of the information, statistics, and stories that you'll read in this book.

But above all, I tried to communicate to these groups and individuals one important truth: that Fouad Masri is the problem. Fouad Masri is a sinner. Because I hate, there is evil in this world.

I am the problem, and only Christ is the ultimate solution. My surrender to God in the name of Jesus the Redeemer cleansed me from my sin and renewed my life. I am now able to follow God and find power over sin, for He is at work in my life. But for the grace of God, I could be in the same position as the hijackers of 9/11.

How do you see Muslims? Deep down, do you feel embittered toward them? Do you view them as the enemy, as I did? It is normal to feel angry. However, the Bible says, "In your anger do not sin" (Ephesians 4:26). Hate is a sin. Jihadists, militant Muslims, are acting only on what the Quran teaches them. They know neither Jesus nor the teachings of the Bible.

Will you take time right now to let God examine your heart? Ask Him about your motives, your values, and your desires. Are you part of the problem, too? Have you harbored hatred that you need to confess? If so, there is good news. Jesus came as a doctor to heal only those who are sick. If you are a murderer in your heart, as I was, I'm thankful to be able to say: The doctor is in.

God is near. Jesus can cleanse you from your guilt and shame.

In Attitude

Our heavenly Father, You alone are holy and pure. I am neither, but You can sanctify me and purify me. Forgive my sin of hatred. Forgive my choices to live by my law rather than Your law. I come to You, the Great Physician, asking You to cleanse me from my sin, for the sake of Christ the Redeemer. I ask this for the sake of Jesus.

Chapter Two

Welcome to the Muslim World

If you have traveled anywhere in the Middle East, you've seen and heard the imprints of Islam everywhere. Stirring you awake at night is the whining *adhan* or call to prayer coming from a minaret's loudspeaker, not far from your hotel. The women's long *jilbabs* and tightly-wrapped headscarves accord with Islamic clothing standards. Even the language is pervaded with *hamdulillahs* ("thanks to God") after sneezing, *bismallahs* ("in the name of God") before eating, and *inshallahs* ("if God wills") when making plans.

At face value, Islam can seem exotic to Westerners, who sometimes become fascinated with the disciplined prayers of some Muslims and taken aback by the sense of piety that pervades religious acts and even business and social situations. The often courteous and hospitable behavior found in Muslim societies endears us to the people. The use of God's name on every lip and in every conversation makes Muslims seem closely obedient to God—"submitted," as a Muslim might describe it. All of this order to life and family can seem attractive to those not otherwise familiar with Islam and its associations.

However, to most Westerners, Islam isn't attractive or exotic, but repulsive. Citizens of the United States and parts of Europe have experienced acts of Islamic terrorism, so we look with anger and disgust upon the Islam that motivates terrorists to kill. We bristle with indignation at social injustices against women—like child marriage and female genital mutilation (FGM)—and we grow cold with fear when watching the angry mobs on television chanting "Death to America!"

As far as religious systems go, Islam comes with certain advantages. Its intricate structure—on a par with any other world religious system—takes much of the guesswork out of living. It governs in detail every aspect of life and possesses an internal logic that claims to answer every question. A Muslim is not expected to question or disobey the Quran or the teachings of the *imams*. Islam as a religion also controls governments and social systems, resulting in fear in the hearts of citizens who want to investigate other religions or question the teachings of Islam. However, it's downright petty to judge Muslims on the basis of their dress, the way they talk, or other cultural customs and habits; they are simply living out the traditions passed on to them.

But what, really, is Islam, and what effect does it have on the societies it pervades? Is there more to Islam than we see on the surface via the news media? Which is the appropriate response to the Muslim world—fascination or fear?

Let me start by saying that individual Muslims are not the problem. Muslims today are the *victims* of a religious and ideological system that locks them in, controlling the subjects they are allowed to investigate, the questions they can ask—even the thoughts they dare to think. I do not believe an appropriate response to individual Muslims is either fascination or fear. Rather, they should have our compassion. The typical Muslim is in many respects just like you, but he or she is held captive by several factors, which this chapter will address in detail—namely, misinformation, limited personal choice, prohibition against questioning the system, and the ever-looming threat of Islam as a political system.

CULTURAL POINTER
Worldview

Because you and your friend have a different religious and cultural background, your worldviews will be different. Simply put, a worldview is the way an individual or group looks at life and reality.

Your friend may do or say something that seems contrary to what you expect. Perhaps you are looking at their action through your own worldview, but in his or her context, that action might make sense.

How can you discover your friend's worldview? Ask many questions. This will help you learn where your friend is coming from and lead towards a deeper relationship. Good questions can help you understand not just worldview, but also feelings, needs, and aspirations—touching the heart, and not just the mind. And as you get to know your Muslim friend on a deeper level, won't this help you as you share Christ?

Information Withheld and Manufactured: Robbed of the Truth

I'll never forget the tears of a sweet-hearted woman named Angela. She served on one of Crescent Project's short-term mission trips to the Muslim world. She was sharing with two young Sunni Muslim women about the birth of Christ, the angels' pronouncement to the shepherds, and the three gifts of the kings from the East.

Afterward I noticed tears in her eyes, and I asked her why she was sad. "They've never heard or read the Christmas story," she answered. "I grew up knowing all about the shepherds, the wise men, the angels, the manger. I loved it. And I sing every year in our church's Christmas program. I thought everyone on earth had heard the story. But they never have?"

Most Muslims live their entire lives so enveloped by Islamic teaching and culture that they never have a chance to learn any of the Bible's truth. I couldn't believe the first Lebanese guy who told me, in all

LEARNING THE ROPES

Ask good questions. In your conversations, ask questions about your Muslim friend's life, culture, family, history, festivals, likes, and dislikes. This is the only way to find out what he or she believes. Don't assume anything...ask!

- What country are you from?
- Tell me about your home country.
- What did you like and dislike about growing up there?
- How long have you been in this country?
- What do you like about this country?
- What did you like about being raised a Muslim?
- What was one difficult experience as a child?
- Did you know any Christians growing up? What was your opinion of them?
- How do you practice your religion? Which practices mean the most to you personally?
- What holidays (or *eids*) do you participate in? What do they mean to you?
- Why do you think there are different religions?
- Who is Jesus, in your opinion? How did you learn this about Jesus?
- What have you heard about Jesus? How do you know those statements are true?
- Have you read the *Injeel* (New Testament)—the revelation of Jesus?

seriousness, that Islam was the original religion, and that Judaism and Christianity came later. We were standing in the Lebanese American University discussing politics and religion—two subjects Muslims *love* to talk about. I'll grant that he knew his politics, but he needed a lesson or two on the history of religion.

I love it when Muslims make such claims. A brief venture into any commonly accepted history book will quickly reveal the lie. A Shi'ite Muslim named Hassan once told me that the *Injeel*—the New Testament—has been changed since God originally gave it. After I guided him through a series of questions to ask his *imam*—questions that we will discuss in a later chapter—Hassan returned to me, downcast, and confessed, "Fouad, my *imam* is confused. He doesn't know the Bible or history."

The Muslim world has an information crisis. Many Muslims hold to beliefs that are simply untrue. How can this be?

First, Muslim governments and religious institutions control their citizens'—even their leaders'—access to information, resulting in profound misunderstandings about the West. Due to Internet censorship and limited outside influences, the Islamic world at large hears only what its leaders allow. They receive only partial and skewed stories about current events, history of the East or the West, and most important, the gospel.

If I were with you in person, I'd show you my Arabic Bible. It's covered in worn brown leather, a gift from my pastor in Lebanon. But there's something strange about this Bible. It is banned in Saudi Arabia. Also in Kuwait, Yemen, Sudan, Libya, and Morocco.

What is wrong with this picture? I can get a Quran at any major bookstore in America. I can even order a free Quran from one of several Islamic websites and have it delivered to my door in a matter of weeks.[1] Yet I have to smuggle my personal Bible into some Muslim-majority countries, and some governments go so far as to persecute anyone who owns or carries the Book of Jesus. (And the media chants its mantra: "Islam is a peaceful religion.")

Why ban the Bible? By doing so, Muslim leaders ensure that their citizens remain ignorant regarding other religions. The majority of Muslims have not read their own holy book, the Quran, and most will never see a page of the New Testament. Since illiteracy is a problem for many Muslims—especially for women—and their exposure to the Quran is usually by hearing it chanted, rather than reading it, they are heavily dependent on their *imams* to guide them.

Second, not only are Muslims deprived of certain information—they are also fed blatant misinformation. The Muslim world on the whole has been schooled in the

SEE ALSO...
To learn more about conversing with a Muslim about the integrity of the Bible, see Chapter 9.

basics of Islam, yet individuals are grossly misled regarding other religions and the West. As I traveled across the Muslim world, I was shocked by what Muslims believe about Christians and even sometimes about their own religion. Most Muslims are taught that Islam preceded Christianity and Judaism; that Christians worship three gods; that the New Testament has been changed since God first gave it; and that "Christian" society—that is, the West—is immoral and godless.

Many Muslims are kind and pious and are seeking to follow God. They have no other spiritual input apart from the untruths they hear from their *imams* at the mosque every week. They are simply regurgitating what they have been taught.

But these beliefs, even if received innocently, can be deadly. A rumor was circulated in the Muslim world in 2005 that a Quran had been flushed down a toilet by Guantanamo Bay guards. The information, beginning as a small paragraph in *Newsweek* magazine, incensed Muslims. *Newsweek* later retracted the statement and apologized, affirming that the rumor was false, but not before anti-America demonstrations left as many as fifteen dead and several others injured. All this because of an unconfirmed rumor.[2]

The best example of both withheld and manufactured information is in the way Muslims view the Bible. Given the Bible's limited availability, when misinformation is spread about its origin and authenticity, the common person has no source by which to verify or refute what he or she has been told. The most common fallacy is that the Quran has come to replace the Bible—something that the Quran never claims. In fact, the Muslim holy book clearly states that it came to *confirm* the earlier messages of prophets like Moses, David, and Jesus, and that these messages were sent by God Almighty. In a later chapter we'll investigate in greater depth the many fallacies that Islamic teachers perpetuate about Christian doctrines, along with ways to counter them.

And the third component of the information crisis is that most Christians today are not going to Muslims to inform them of the truth. There are only three missionaries (to Muslims) for every million Muslims.

And the majority of Muslims coming to the West never visit a Christian home. The need is urgent for followers of Jesus not only to proclaim to Muslims the teachings of Christ, but also to help correct their misunderstandings about Christianity. In fact, as we will discuss later, often the misinformation must be corrected before we can impart the truth.

Lack of Personal Choice: Decided in the Delivery Room

The second problem that traps Muslims within a locked-in system is the lack of personal freedom of religion. Islam claims, not only that it is a way of life, but that it is the *best* way of life, and the *only* option available to those born in a Muslim community. Everything from schooling to washing, from sports to the clothes Muslims wear must be controlled by Islam as defined by the *Sunnah* (teachings based on the life of Muhammad) and as interpreted by one's religious leaders.

When a child is born to Muslim parents, his worldview has been decided for him—it is Islam. Within minutes after the baby is born, the father or grandfather whispers the *Shahadah*, the Islamic creed—"There is no god but Allah, and Muhammad is the messenger of Allah"—in the baby's ear, thus making him a Muslim. (In the same way, if a person wants to convert to Islam, he need only recite the *Shahadah* in the presence of another Muslim, and he becomes a Muslim.)

In the West, parents sometimes raise their child without any particular faith, in hopes that the child will "find her own path." Or they may expose her equally to different world religions, believing it best that their child know all the options and choose the religion that fits her best. These parents feel that they have no right to pressure their children into a worldview or religion.

This parenting style is virtually nonexistent in the Muslim world. One's identity as a Muslim is woven through the fabric of society, into every sphere of life—marriage and family, education, and politics. Individuals are identified as Muslims from birth to old age.

But what about mixed marriages, where one spouse is Christian and the other Muslim? Or the rare case when one spouse is Jewish or Hindu, and the other Muslim? In Islam, the religion of the father determines the religious upbringing of the children. And since Muslim women are forbidden to marry non-Muslims, in practically every case children from a "half-Muslim" family will be considered Muslims.

This issue came to the forefront during President Barack Obama's campaign, when leaders from Islamic countries called the future United States' president "our Muslim brother." Whether or not Barack Hussein Obama considers himself a Muslim now, the fact that his father was a Muslim (from Kenya) is all that most Muslims require in order to automatically consider him one...from birth to death, through and through. (By the way, President Obama's repeated claims that he is a Christian provide us the opportunity to use him as an example as we help our friends follow Christ.)

Thankfully, America still allows freedom of religion, and even those born here to Muslim families do not have to be defined by Islam their entire lives. Many Muslims have become Christians. However, the reality for many Muslims worldwide is that personal choice in matters of religion is out of reach. This lack of freedom further binds them to the system of Islam.

Prohibition Against Questions and Doubt: An Islam Above Critique

In 2007, a young Egyptian man, Nabil, was sentenced to four years in prison in Alexandria. Why? He criticized Al-Azhar University, a renowned Islamic institution, on his online blog. He posted his negative opinions about a strict version of Islam, criticizing Al-Azhar University of "spreading racial ideas" and "suppressing free thought."

Nabil calls himself a secular Muslim (a title whose self-contradiction always amuses me). Nabil represents a growing number of Muslims fighting for a voice. They are ready for change but aren't sure where to turn. In fact, most Muslims who leave Islam turn to secularism because no one has shared with them the truth of Christ and His teachings. Like Nabil, they may remain culturally Muslim, but can no longer subscribe to the Islamic belief system. They remain unaware of any better option.

Nabil's imprisonment emphasizes the third force that victimizes Muslims—the prohibition against questioning, or even doubting, the tenets of their religion, their prophet, and the Quran. The Quran is seen to be above textual criticism, the prophet above any moral critique, and Islam the absolute purest religion, in need of no modification.

This was further illustrated when a young Asian Muslim woman, Safia, was caught by her Muslim roommate reading the Bible at a university in the United States. The roommate told their student association on campus, and the other Muslims joined in ostracizing Safia, refusing to sit at the same table with her. They viewed Safia's Bible reading as questioning or doubting Islam. If Islam is the best way of life, why would one seek anything outside it? Collective reprimands, group shaming, and public expressions of displeasure are common ways to "discipline" members of the Muslim community who take interest in anything outside of Islam.

Hanan Arzay, a fifteen-year-old Muslim student in New York, requested literal interpretations of the Islamic holy books from her Quran teacher. Both the teacher and fellow students threw chalk at her for the request. Hanan was kicked out of two Islamic schools before turning to an underground punk Muslim community, which she says saved her faith.[3]

Nabil turned to secularism and criticized the suppression of free thought. Safia turned to the teachings of Jesus Christ and read a Bible someone had given her. Hanan asked honest questions and ended up in a Muslim subculture. In every case, no matter what doubts or criticisms these young Muslims expressed, they were publicly shamed by the community.

In Christianity, the doubt of a seeking heart is a virtue. In Islam, doubt is a sin. Thomas, though one of Christ's disciples, was a doubter (see John 20:24–29). But Christ's post-resurrection treatment of Thomas was not public shame and humiliation. He didn't kick Thomas out of the group, but offered proof of His bodily resurrection and included him. Jesus saw through Thomas's doubts to his search for faith and rewarded him. Sincere questioning and searching for answers receives God's favor and will lead to the truth.

The scientific method is innately skeptical; it is based on asking more and more questions, which eventually lead to answers. Tests are repeated until the problem is solved. But Muslims do not allow this empirical method as a tool for evaluating the religion of Islam. In fact, Islam considers doubt a sin punishable by death. The prophet dictated one set way to live; if Muhammad said, "Bow," the Muslim may never ask, "Why?" but only, "How low?" To doubt the prophet or his message is to doubt God Himself. So a worldwide community of Muslims lives continually in the dark, shielded from any biblical ideas.

Muslim Civil Authority: Islam as a Political System

Lina Joy, a Muslim-born Malaysian woman, came to know Christ as a young woman. In order to marry her Christian fiancé, she appealed to her government to change her religious affiliation on a government-issued identification card from "Islam" to "Christianity." In 2007, Malaysia's highest court rejected Lina Joy's battle to be legally recognized as a Christian. Even though she began following Jesus almost twenty years earlier, in the eyes of the government, Lina remains Muslim.[4]

For ethnic Malays, there's only one religious option: Islam. Like many other Islamic states, the Malaysian government officially grants freedom of religion, but declares that all ethnic Malays are permanently Muslim. No room exists for discussion. A Malaysian chief justice at Lina's hearing said, "She cannot at her own whim simply enter or leave her religion.... She must follow rules."[5]

This outright discrimination reveals the truth about Islam's role in Malaysia and many other Muslim-majority states. Islam here has become more of a *political system* than a *spiritual system*. If Islam was strictly a religious system, and a follower betrayed God by leaving the religion, then God should be the ultimate just judge of that person. The apostate's offense was against God, not against civil authority. But if a person betrays his country, that is another matter. The betrayer of his homeland must be punished by fellow countrymen. So when Islamic governments persecute and even execute a person because of his spiritual values or choice of religion, they are demonstrating that Islam is in reality a political system.

The religious logic behind Islam's disallowance of conversion is that this might encourage others to do the same. If the government can bar its citizens from changing their religion, or shame them enough when they do, others won't dare to convert. This pressure keeps Muslims from investigating other religions or publicly acknowledging their belief in Christ. But the dictates of political leadership are, by definition, political, not religious; Islam that is enforced by civil authority is shown to be a political system.

What happens to Muslims who do acknowledge Christ in these countries? Any Muslim who identifies himself as a Christian brings upon himself the law of *Ridda*. According to this component of Islamic *Shariah* code, a convert from Islam to any other religion has three days to return to Islam or must face execution. This not only applies to Muslims living under Islamic governments; it is also technically true (though obviously difficult to enforce) for any Muslim who becomes a Christian, even in the "free" West.

The Leaky Roof

These four factors are the primary reasons I don't see individual Muslims as the problem, but as victims of a restrictive system. With

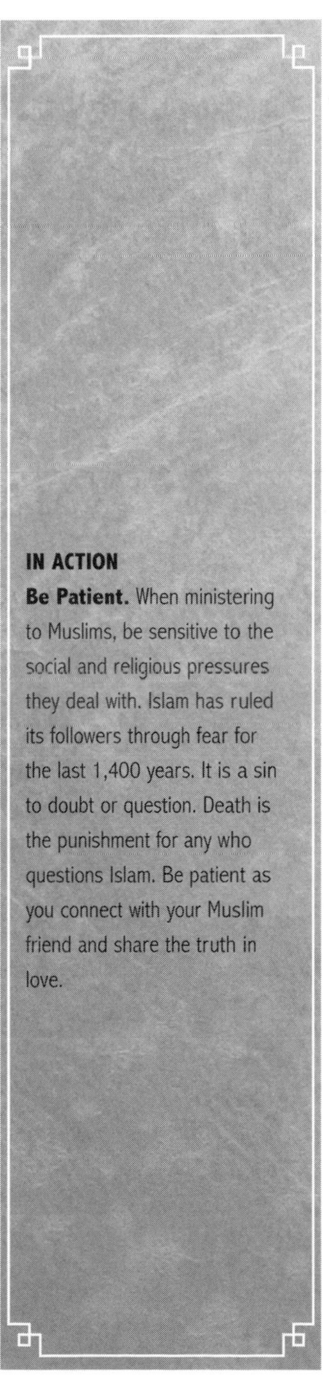

IN ACTION

Be Patient. When ministering to Muslims, be sensitive to the social and religious pressures they deal with. Islam has ruled its followers through fear for the last 1,400 years. It is a sin to doubt or question. Death is the punishment for any who questions Islam. Be patient as you connect with your Muslim friend and share the truth in love.

Muslim governments and religious leaders doing all they can to shame and intimidate their communities, it is no wonder that many Muslims will never explore beyond Islam. They'll never ask, "Is there more to God than religion?"

A Libyan student and I were talking when he acknowledged, "We Muslims know we have problems. You see, living in the Islamic world is like living in a house with a leaky roof. Even though the roof leaks, I'd rather be in the house than be outside in the rain."

For many Muslims, staying within the bounds of Islam is merely an exercise in pragmatism. They do not want to go against family, culture, or country. Why should they, since they firmly believe that no other viable option exists? They would rather keep the peace with their culture, even if that means living with the problems and dilemmas they face in Islam. They put up with the leaks, preferring to bail water with buckets, rather than question their house's security or venture outside in search of other shelters.

Even those living in our culture usually walk in uninformed darkness. If we don't share with them, who will? Certainly their Muslim governments and *imams* won't let them in on the good news. If we don't tell Muslims, they will live their lives in a house that we know has worse problems than a leaky roof—it's perched on the edge of a cliff, certain to slide off into Christless eternity.

The barriers that keep Muslims from knowing and following Jesus might intimidate us who are followers of Christ, and frighten us away from sharing with them. But I urge you to respond with compassion, not fear. Take heart—Muslims are coming to the secure shelter of Jesus, and these Muslim-background Christians are living and speaking boldly, taking a stand for Jesus and His gospel.

It is our mandate to show Muslims the way to a house of eternal life and joy—the house that is Jesus'.

ℵ

In Attitude

Our heavenly Father, I thank You for sending Jesus to be the Savior of all humanity. I ask that government leaders of nations and communities around the world would allow the Bible to be read, that all might learn of Your salvation.

Forgive me for succumbing to a spirit of fear and avoidance of Muslims. I pray You will change my heart and give me a spirit of compassion, that I might become Your instrument in leading Muslims to You, the giver of eternal life. I ask this for the sake of Jesus.

Chapter Three

The Spiritual Sahara

In Arabic, *Islam* literally means "to surrender," and a *Muslim* is "one who surrenders"—that is, surrenders to Allah through the teachings of Muhammad.

Today more than seven million Muslims live in North America and 1.3 billion worldwide. The majority of them are still waiting for an authentic Christian witness. The Bible is banned in many Muslim countries, and many don't have complete freedom to investigate other religions and learn about Jesus. Few of them will ever hear the message. The majority of Muslim international students in the United States and Canada will never visit a Christian home throughout the duration of their studies.

Ahmad was an international student from Saudi Arabia. When I met him, I asked what he thought of America after having lived here a few months. He replied, "It is a bad country."

I queried further, "What do you think of Christianity after living here?"

"That is what makes America a bad country," Ahmad said. "Because Christianity is a bad religion."

I was surprised that Ahmad was being so honest with me; I wanted to hear more. I knew he had never read the Bible (it is banned in Saudi Arabia), so I was curious why he had such a low opinion of Christianity. I didn't have to ask; he went ahead and told me. He said that the previous week in class students were passing around a Christian publication called *Playboy*.

LEARNING THE ROPES

Attend an Islamic or cultural event. Go to an Arab-American festival, a Persian film festival, or an *Eid-ul-Fitr* end of Ramadan celebration at a mosque. These events can be excellent learning experiences, and provide topics for conversations later. "Do you have any other films from your country that I could see?" "What does the Ramadan fast mean to you?"

"But *Playboy* is not a religious magazine at all," I said.

He wasn't convinced. In Ahmad's mind, just as all Saudi Arabians are Muslim, so all Americans are Christians. "The girls in *Playboy* are Americans," was his objection. Therefore, *Playboy* was a Christian magazine.

Muslims today look to secular Western culture—our television, movies, music, Internet, and magazines—for their definition of Christian values. Who will counter the message of Hollywood and share instead the true values of the Bible? Who will break through the barriers of Islam and untangle the mixed messages that Muslims like Ahmad are receiving about Christianity? The good news is, despite all the factors heavily weighted against them, Muslims are coming to know the Savior. In spite of the misinformation that turns them off, Muslims are still open to the gospel.

It's a Free Country

I have found that Muslims in the West are more open than ever to the message of Jesus. For immigrants and students coming from restrictive Muslim countries, the freedom they enjoy opens the door to investigate new thoughts and religions. Though some Muslims use their newfound freedom for ill, others use it to read the New Testament, learn from Christian friends, and seek Jesus Christ. When authentic followers of Christ share with Muslims within the natural relationships the Holy Spirit provides, miracles happen.

A phone conversation I had with a complete stranger helped me realize the great openness of Muslims in America. The phone rang at my house, and I heard a female voice on the other end offering the traditional Muslim greeting, "*Assalamu-alaykum*." I answered with the proper response and was immediately asked, "Where are you from, brother?"

"I'm from Lebanon. Where are you from, sister?"

"I'm from Sudan."

Surprised, I asked the woman if she was calling me from Sudan. She said no, but she worked for a phone company in Virginia, and they were offering new calling rates to Lebanon. Was I interested?

"I don't want to change my calling plan," I said, "but tell me, how long have you been in Virginia?"

Three months, she answered.

"Have you read the *Injeel*?"

"I'm a Muslim!" she exclaimed.

"A Muslim? *Al-hamdulillah!* [Praise God!]" I continued with a series of statements, and she emphatically agreed with each one:

- "Muslims believe in one God." Yes.
- "Muslims believe God sent Jesus." Yes.
- "Muslims believe God sent the *Injeel*." Yes.

CULTURAL POINTER

***Eid al-Adha:* The Feast of Sacrifice**

Every year Muslims around the world celebrate the feast of *Eid al-Adha*, also known as the Feast of Sacrifice or Great Feast *(Eid ul-Kabir)*, in Southeast Asia as *Bakr Eid*, and in the Turkic world as *Kurban Bayram*. At this time, many Muslims sacrifice a sheep or goat to commemorate how God redeemed the son of Abraham, as recorded in the Quran (37:99-113).

However, the Bible affirms that just as God redeemed the son of Abraham with the sacrifice of the ram He provided, so God redeemed the world through the blood of Jesus Christ. Jesus became the true *Adha:* He was the Lamb of God, sacrificed to set us free from sin, by which God bridged the gulf that separated us from Him. Christians celebrate the once-for-all sacrifice of Jesus Christ every Easter.

Then I asked, "Would you like to read the *Injeel*, since this is a free country?"

She said yes! So I wrote down her address and FedEx'd an Arabic *Injeel* to her as a welcome gift to America. The Sudanese woman on the phone was living in a country where she could read the book of Jesus and make her own decision about it.

In my suburb, a group of Muslims purchased a church and redesigned it as a mosque. (Incidentally, in Muslim countries no mosques are allowed to be bought and remodeled to become churches.) I drive by that mosque regularly and pray for the worshipers there. Recently, a man was giving a presentation on Jesus in the Quran at the mosque, so of course I attended.

The speaker tried his best to talk about Jesus in the Quran, but his source material was limited. Although the Quran contains ninety-three references to Jesus, only a few of them describe His life and teachings. After the presentation and the *Juma'a* (Friday noon gathering) message, I thanked the speaker and asked if I could give him the Arabic-English New Testament.

"I have never seen the *Injeel* side by side in two languages," he told me. He thanked me and promised to read it.

These stories are not isolated. Our ministry supplies hundreds of *Injeels* every year, each of them given to a Muslim by a Christian friend. The openness of Muslims in the "free" West is so great, even teachers and religious leaders in mosques are thankful to read the *Injeel* of Jesus. Make no mistake—countless Muslims are searching for Christ, making use of their freedom in the West. Will we make use of ours?

A Spiritual Desert of Unanswered Questions

I've pointed out the advantages of Islam as a religious system, but it falls short where mere "systems" often do—in the areas of critical importance. Unanswered questions leave Muslims wandering through a spiritual desert, their hunger never satisfied, their thirst never quenched. *Can I be cured of my sin and shame? If so, how? Where will I spend eternity? How can my character change? Is there proof for the resurrection of the dead? Do good works satisfy God's holiness? When will I have done enough good works?*

In the absence of answers, Muslims deal with these nagging questions in different ways. Some devoted Muslims try to numb their fears with good works, turning to Islamic ritual duties, like prayer ceremonies, chanting of the Quran, and fasting. Others abandon the practice of Islam and turn to secularism and materialism to medicate their souls.

Today, more than ever, the call to the community of Jesus is to reach out a hand to hungry, searching Muslims. From the outside we may think Muslims are content in their self-contained world. But anyone who gains a glimpse into the individual Muslim's personal inner workings will see that they inhabit a spiritual wilderness. They long for direction. I pray that we will see our Muslim neighbors wandering the desert that is Islam and will compassionately answer the cry of John the Baptist:

Prepare the way of the Lord,
make his paths straight.
Every valley shall be filled,
and every mountain and hill shall be made low,
and the crooked shall become straight,
and the rough places shall become level ways,
and all flesh shall see the salvation of God.
—Luke 3:4-6, ESV

No Reliable Cure for Sin

You never have to convince Muslims that they are guilty of sin. They readily admit to experiencing shame and guilt. But Islam never offers any reliable solution for this desperate problem. If a Muslim is honest with himself, he hopes his good deeds will cover over his sin, but he can never have certainty. He has no choice but to bear his shame quietly.

While sharing my personal testimony with a man named Khaled in Morocco, I told him that Jesus saved me from the hatred that was in my heart toward Palestinians and Israelis. Jesus had renewed my heart so that I now prayed for the same people I had once hated. Khaled interrupted me at this point in my testimony and asked me what I thought was an unrelated question. "Have you ever read the Holy Quran?"

"Yes," I answered. "I've read it fourteen times—in Arabic."

Khaled continued, "I've read it twice, but I've never found a cure for sin."

My friend Khaled had stumbled upon one of the most important unanswered questions in Islam. He understood the stain of sin, but had never heard of a way to become confidently clean. "Maybe" is the word hanging over Muslims worldwide. *On Judgment Day will my good works erase my bad works*. Islam answers, "Maybe."

(And, by the way, the God of the Bible answers this question, "No. Only My Son's death is payment enough for your debt.")

SEE ALSO...

To learn more about how to converse with a Muslim about salvation and security in Christ, see Chapter 10.

Eternity: Heaven or Hell?

The second unanswered question is related to the first. In Islam, no one can be assured of their eternal destiny. On Judgment Day, God judges humanity according to each person's good works and religious beliefs. However, Islam's view of God's sovereignty—in reality a whimsical and unpredictable form of "fate"—leaves Muslims with a deeply unsettling lack of assurance. Islam teaches that God reserves the right to change His mind...*no matter what you've done or believed*.

According to Islamic traditions, three questions will be asked of every person on the Day of Judgment: *Who is your Lord? Who is your prophet?* and *What is your religion?* Muslims believe that on earth one's own mind controls his or her tongue, but on Judgment Day, God controls the tongue. Therefore, each individual will answer the three questions according to God's capricious decision, and each person's fate—heaven or hell—will be determined based on these answers.

This, of course, is contrary to the promise in our Bible that those who believe in and confess Jesus Christ will not be disappointed. The message in Romans 10:9-10 is clear: "If you confess with your mouth, 'Jesus is Lord,' and believe in your heart that God raised him from the dead, you will be saved. For it is with your heart that you believe and are justified, and it is with your mouth that you confess and are saved." And in 1 John 1:9, "If we confess our sins, he is faithful and just and will forgive us our sins and purify us from all unrighteousness."

A Change in Character

When Aasiyah Hassan was beheaded in New York state in February 2009 and her husband was charged with her murder, women's organizations rightly designated it an "honor killing."[6] (Days earlier, Aasiyah had presented her husband with divorce papers, thus dishonoring the family in the eyes of Islam. According to Islamic tradition, an honor killing removes the "sinner's" shame from the family and restores their honor.) But the story goes deeper than that: Muzaammil "Mo" Hassan and his wife Aasiya were founders of the Bridges TV cable channel, which was intended to break down stereotypes against Muslims in America. While Islamic leaders insisted Aasiya's murder was nonreligious in nature, no one is fooled, and the irony is lost on no one. Mo has since been convicted and sentenced to twenty-five years to life,[7] thus substantiating the exact stereotypes he set out to dispel. He claims that Muslims exhibit a peaceful character, but he himself has manifested a character of gruesome violence.

At its core, Islam offers no way to change one's character, to offer new life and a fresh beginning. Jesus alone can transform someone into a new creation. In fact, He told Nicodemus that one must be born again in order to enter God's kingdom. Although Islam claims to be a religion of the heart, the rampant reality of excessive social injustices, vengeances, and prejudices in the Muslim world testify that the religion of Islam does not develop godly character. Islam has failed to change the values of its adherents. Our Lord said we would distinguish God's true followers from all others by their fruit—their actions (see Matthew 7:20).

In contrast, when Muslims see and receive authentic forgiveness, everything changes. I know two different Muslims, both named Ali and both from Iran, who experienced forgiveness and were never the same again.

The first Ali was watching a news report on television about a police officer who was shot in the line of duty. As the officer emerged from his coma, he told the interviewer, "I forgive the man who shot me." Ali was incredulous. How could the first words on this officer's lips be ones of kindness toward his would-be killer? How could he forgive? The man's example eventually led to Ali's investigation and acceptance of Christ's forgiveness.

The second Ali could not hide from his guilt and sin. He repeatedly drank alcohol—a serious offense in Islam—and beat his wife in his drunken rages. He was sorry for his waywardness but had nowhere to turn. He even participated in the *Hajj*—the pilgrimage to Mecca. The *Hajj* didn't change Ali, but when he encountered the risen Christ in a dream, he was forever transformed. The Holy Spirit began altering Ali's life and character, until his experience of God's grace spilled over and he asked forgiveness from wife.

How can our hearts be changed? Only by the grace of God.

Become an Answer to Someone's Prayer

We've examined three of the many life-critical questions for which Islam has no adequate answers. Your Muslim friends desperately need your sympathy and compassion; their religion falls sadly short in addressing their deepest human needs. They are living in a desolate spiritual terrain like the one described in John the Baptist's cry. The rough places in their understanding of God—you have the opportunity to smooth them. Valleys of misinformation about Christianity need to be filled in by your authentic witness. You can help bring low the daunting mountains of fear and isolation, in order that Muslims might walk in peace with the Savior.

Devout Muslims pray to God daily, "Show us the straight path." Jesus said, "I am the way." He is the path that Muslims need. Could it be that God is calling you to clear the way for the Messiah Jesus to enter the life of your Muslim friend? Only Christ can answer the plea of Muslims worldwide and lead them in the straight path.

> *"I am the way and the truth and the life. No one comes to the Father except through me."*
> —Jesus in John 14:6

In Attitude

Our heavenly Father, You are my light and my salvation, I praise You for taking the initiative to bring life to us, for we would never have come to You by ourselves. Break my heart for Muslims who hunger and thirst for You, and make my life a tool in Your hand to prepare the way of the Lord. I ask this for the sake of Jesus.

Chapter Four

Crisis in the Church

During my time in seminary, I served in the youth program at our fifteen-year-old church. We were committed to teenagers in the church, but we also wanted to spread the Word and invite teenagers from the community. We started small. We walked a four-block radius surrounding the church's location and passed out flyers about an upcoming event. To our dismay, we discovered that most of the neighbors in this four-block radius didn't even know a church existed in their neighborhood. A lady one block away said, "Oh, I thought that was a daycare center."

How can a church worship for fifteen years in one location and not make itself known? If we have so little impact on our nearest neighbors, how can we expect to impact the world?

This problem is not limited to churches in the United States or the West. In Lebanon—a field ripe with many who have never heard the gospel—I became acquainted with one church where few of the members were connecting with their Muslim, Druze, or other unsaved neighbors. When I asked the pastor why he didn't encourage his congregation to get involved in the Great Commission and reach out to these people, he said, "We cannot go, because we *are* the mission field. The missionaries should be sent to us."

> *"All authority in heaven and on earth has been given to me. Therefore go and make disciples of all nations."*
> —Jesus in Matthew 28:18-19

IN ACTION
Go prayerwalking. Prayerwalk in a part of town where you know Muslims live (maybe near a mosque or in your neighborhood). Go with a partner if possible. When you pass a Muslim home, pray for those who live there. Pray for opportunities to meet Muslims on your walk. Pray for a spiritual awakening in their hearts and in their countries.

IN ACTION
Befriend the lonely. Many international students are Muslims. Holidays can be lonely times for them, great opportunities to invite them for a meal or a family game night. Or maybe once a month host an international Muslim student in your home. Learn more about his life, classes, and friends, and seek to be his "home away from home."

Jesus spoke these words to His followers two thousand years ago, yet today there are still billions among the "nations" who have never seen a page of the New Testament or heard the teachings of Christ. Did the disciples fail? No, they expended their lives for the sake of the gospel, its message reaching as far as Asia, Rome, Spain, India, and Africa.

The early church did not fail Jesus' mandate. The failure is largely due to the church's lack of obedience in later centuries, including this one. And Muslims are one of the largest people groups we have let down. Our lack of obedience has left Muslims suffering as victims of an oppressive system, bound in sin, misinformed about Christ and His teachings. The church's misunderstanding of Muslims and unwillingness to go past its safe boundaries has kept them from experiencing the true peace and joy that Christ offers freely.

That is the cost of our complacency. And that's why reaching Muslims should matter to us.

What Is the Church?

The Bible defines the church as the community that has taken Jesus of Nazareth to be the promised Messiah—the only Savior from sin and the risen Lord of all. The Greek word *ekklesia*, rendered by most Bible scholars as "church," literally means "called out" or "a gathering of those who are called out."

Why do these gatherings exist? Among other purposes, God expects the community of Christians to represent Jesus' teachings by modeling how God can change lives—lives of believers in the church and lives around us. Also, the church is meant to transform the culture in which it finds itself. It transforms the moral fabric of a culture by powerful, Spirit-driven influence. Furthermore, the church worships and lifts up the name of Christ on earth, making Him known everywhere.

But more than anything else, the church exists on earth to widely sow the message of Christ and reproduce itself again and again in new places and new ways. It is designed to multiply. In order to fulfill this purpose, the church must necessarily have a presence on earth, rather than just in heaven. We who have been saved from our sins eagerly anticipate eternity, where every tear will be wiped from every face. But meanwhile we remain in this life for a purpose—to share our eternal hope with others.

The nations urgently need to hear the life-transforming truth of Jesus. The news headlines bear ample testimony to the world's disastrous condition: war, genocide, racism, slavery, sexual immorality, and greed run rampant in all societies. Our mission is to proclaim the word of faith and life: "That if you confess with your mouth,

The church is the hands and feet of Christ. We are the mirror that reflects the light of Christ —Fouad Masri

You will be my witnesses! —Jesus in Acts 1:8

The family of Jesus invites all to the table. —Fouad Masri

IN ACTION

Christians should not criticize one another.

Refrain from putting down other Christians, denominations, or ministries. Even though some Christian leaders have been negative towards Islam and Muslims, we must remain positive as we interact with our Muslim friend. You can explain that in Christianity, people are allowed to share their opinions freely. However, always bring the focus back to the Biblical teachings of Christ and not controversies.

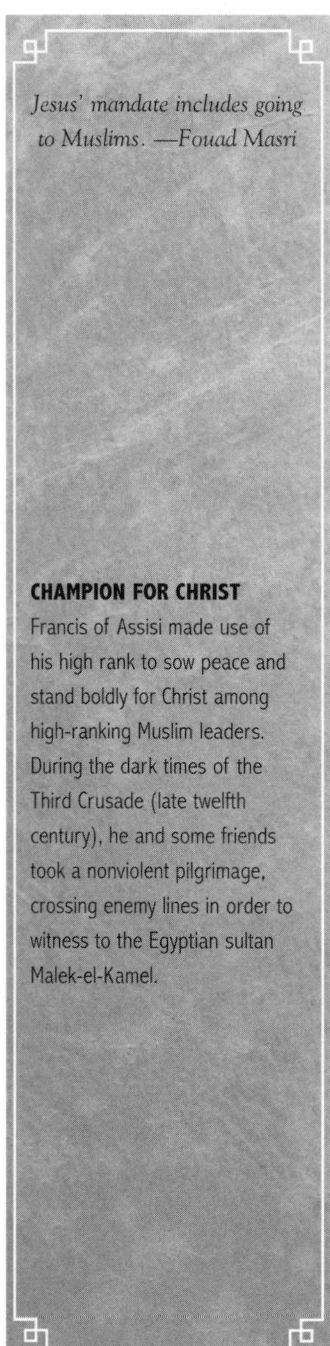

'Jesus is Lord,' and believe in your heart that God raised him from the dead, you will be saved" (Romans 10:9). And, "If we confess our sins, he is faithful and just and will forgive us our sins and purify us from all unrighteousness" (1 John 1:9). We have a promise. Confession is the way we are saved and enter the family of Jesus. The church is the fellowship of those who are set apart by their confession.

If we simply endure this life without helping others understand and confess this truth, we will have failed our mission. Our life on earth and the opportunities we make and take—the way we interact with each person we meet and the way we conduct our lives before the watching world—it all leads to eternal consequences.

The church is a living and life-giving organism. But we are not operating to our full capacity; we are falling short of our purpose, especially with respect to Muslims. Our mission is in crisis for two reasons: First, we haven't sought to understand Muslims. We've called them militants and terrorists, and we've written them off as unreachable and condemned them without a second glance. And second, we are not going to them. We've ignored them and quietly hoped that their problems would solve themselves. We send and support a token few specialists—the missionaries—but the rest of us are failing to take part in the great mandate of Jesus to take the gospel to Muslims right here where we live.

We Haven't Sought to Understand Muslims

Beirut, Lebanon, the city where I grew up, is in the heart of the 10/40 Window—that is, the portion of the Eastern Hemisphere that falls between ten and forty degrees north latitude. The Window stretches across Africa and Asia, comprising two-thirds of the world's population. Almost all of the fifty-five least-reached countries lie in this region, and most of them are Muslim-majority countries.

Today the church supports fewer than three missionary workers for every one million Muslims. If every Muslim were to hear Christ's message, each worker would be responsible for getting the word out to roughly 300,000 Muslims! Is it any wonder that we're not seeing great numbers of Muslims coming to Christ? We've barely given them a chance.

The greatest fallacy among Christians regarding Muslims is that Muslims are hard to reach. Now if we were providing thousands of Christian missionaries per million Muslims and none were coming to Jesus, then yes, I would agree that Muslims were difficult to evangelize. But we've splashed only a few drops of water on the spiritual desert of Islam, sighing in dismay that the

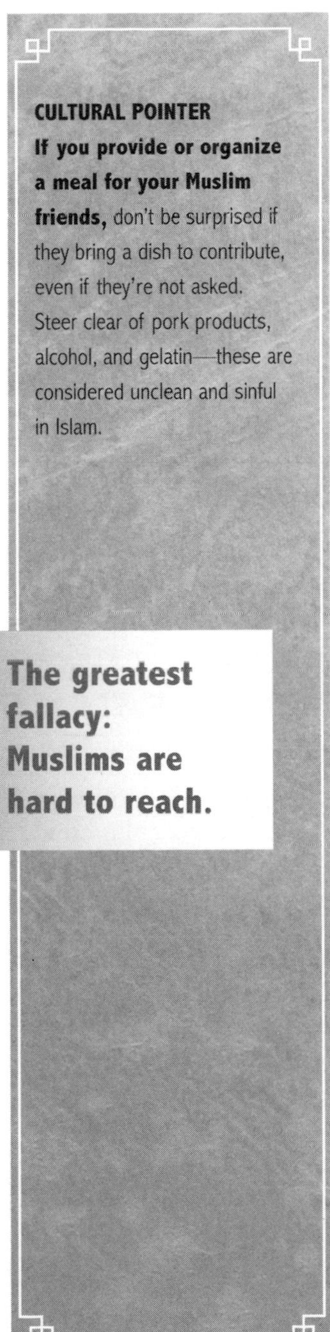

CULTURAL POINTER

If you provide or organize a meal for your Muslim friends, don't be surprised if they bring a dish to contribute, even if they're not asked. Steer clear of pork products, alcohol, and gelatin—these are considered unclean and sinful in Islam.

The greatest fallacy: Muslims are hard to reach.

desert hasn't flourished into a jungle of true faith. Even when Muslims arrive at our borders and in our neighborhood, what do we do? We close the garage door as quickly as possible.

Muslims love to talk about spiritual things.

Don't let the devil's lie sway you or your church. Muslims are not hard to reach. In fact, they are the easiest group when it comes to talking about Jesus. Two things Muslims love to talk about are politics and religion. It's we who are the problem; we're the ones who squirm when these topics come up. Muslims *want* to talk about spiritual things. So let's open up the conversations, and let's always lead them back to Jesus. Your Muslim friends are happy to go there with you.

The truth is, in the last fifteen years more Muslims have become followers of Jesus than in the previous 1400 years combined. Why? Mostly for three reasons: They've either sought and discovered the truth of the Bible for themselves, were touched by the lifestyle of authentic Christians, or had a supernatural dream or vision about Jesus that spurred them to ask more questions. Muslims are not hardened to the gospel. They simply have not heard.[8]

In the past the church's indifference toward Muslims has prevented many from hearing the good news. Even some of our missionaries are not prepared to be effective witnesses for Christ.

When I was a young believer in Lebanon, I met an American missionary who told me he hated Lebanese food. I couldn't help but look surprised. After all, Lebanese food is the food served in heaven! (So the Lebanese say.)

He went on, "You guys always cook with garlic."

Yeah, I thought to myself, *the Lebanese brush their teeth with garlic. What's your point?*

It turns out he had been plucked out of Denver, Colorado, and dropped with little preparation or evaluation into Beirut. He didn't enjoy the people, culture, or language of Lebanon. He didn't have one good thing to say about his experience there. He would have been much more comfortable with a burger than a chicken *shawarma*. I can imagine the way he must have summed up his short stay in Lebanon: "It is so hard to reach Muslims." But he had come with an attitude that guaranteed failure—an attitude that was, no doubt, obvious to every Muslim he met.

Many who could otherwise be effective ambassadors to Muslims are hampered by an alienating us-versus-them mentality. But God's Word says that Muslims aren't "them"—they're more of us! Jesus said, "I have other sheep that are not of this sheep pen. I must bring them also. They too will listen to my voice, and there shall be one flock and one shepherd" (John 10:16). Jesus came to save all ethnicities and nationalities, so that He, our one Shepherd, might gather us all into one fold. The church has dismissed Arabs in particular and Muslims in general far too long, when we should be going out of our way to foster Christ's one-flock unity.

Is it appropriate for us to criticize Muslims for their behavior or their customs? Do we have a right to belittle them for their beliefs? Christ is our example. Jesus never criticized sincere sinners, other religions, or other cultures. The only people he criticized were the hypocrites. So for an ambassador of Christ, criticism is a valid tool, but it must be targeted first toward ourselves, and never toward the seeking unbeliever. Instead, let's work to build bridges with them so that we can then introduce them to the One who can satisfy their deepest longings.

Never forget: We are citizens of heaven, agents of God's love.

We are the ambassadors of Jesus Christ.

We Are Not Going to Them

I'm amazed at the variety of theologies and theories I've discovered among Christians—many of which I lump together as "Little Bo Peep Theology":

Little Bo Peep has lost her sheep
And can't tell where to find them.
Leave them alone, and they'll come home,
Wagging their tails behind them.

This children's nursery rhyme, when applied to our mission to a lost world, describes a passive evangelistic method. Christians who hold a Little Bo Peep view of the gospel think that if we leave the nonbelievers alone, somehow they will eventually hear and believe. In time, people will come wandering back to Jesus, tails wagging happily, and start following His teachings. By some undetermined means, the lost will spontaneously repent and follow Christ.

How starkly this theology contrasts with the example of Jesus, the Good Shepherd who lay down His life for the sheep. He doesn't wait for the wanderer to return; instead, He who came "to seek and save that which was lost" leaves the ninety-nine sheep in the fold in order to actively, passionately search for the one sheep that is lost.

I've known some Christians who think the Great Commission (Matthew 28:18-20) is an option. They think this command is for missionaries. And they're right. But what is a missionary? The word comes from the Latin word for "messenger." Simply put, a missionary is someone who delivers a message. Every follower of Jesus is a person entrusted with His message and mandated to obey His Commission. In other words, every authentic, practicing Christian is a missionary.

When Christ said "Go," He meant "Go! Yes, you!" "Go" means getting out of our comfort zone, reaching out, and taking action on behalf of lost sheep who will never come home on their own. This is a command I must obey if I call myself a follower of Jesus.

Many Christians today believe two things about evangelism—that evangelism is comprised of an activity with a start and stop time, and that evangelism should be performed by evangelists or church pastors. Christians often doubt their ability to evangelize, citing lack of giftedness, or they delegate the task to their church leaders and content themselves with tithing. These mistaken beliefs grow out of a misunderstanding of what it actually is. Evangelism at the most basic level is simply sharing the good news of Jesus Christ with others and leaving the results to God.

"Evangelism" comes from a Greek word that means "to share the good news." Regardless of race, nationality, or religion we want to share the good news with all people. What is this good news? The angel said to the shepherds, "I bring you good news.... Today in the town of David a Savior has been born to you; he is Christ the Lord" (Luke 2:10-11). This great news is that the Savior, the Christ, the Messiah has come. This is the personal faith of every biblical Christian, as taught in the *Injeel* (the New Testament).

Sharing one's faith with a Muslim can often appear like a daunting task, even for the most committed Christian. Regardless of the challenges, the goal of Christians is to be the hands and feet of Christ, and to learn to communicate his message to Muslims effectively. We as Christians are always witnessing through our actions, but it is equally important to be able to convey the gospel clearly with our words.

Many Muslims are only nominal followers of Islam. They have a limited knowledge comprised solely of traditional beliefs about their religion, and often even those who know Islam inside and out still end up leaving it. Christians do not need to be experts in Islam, Islamic history, or the Quran to be effective communicators of the good news of Jesus Christ to Muslims. They just need to know and understand how to use bridges that cross the divide between Christianity and Islam. (More on bridges later.)

Not long after I started Crescent Project, a friend of mine sat me down at Starbucks, looked me in the eye, and told me I should close the ministry's doors. Taken aback, I

> *I am compelled to preach. Woe to me if I do not preach the gospel!... Though I am free and belong to no man, I make myself a slave to everyone, to win as many as possible. To the Jews I became like a Jew, to win the Jews. To those under the law I became like one under the law (though I myself am not under the law), so as to win those under the law. To those not having the law I became like one not having the law (though I am not free from God's law but am under Christ's law), so as to win those not having the law. To the weak I became weak, to win the weak. I have become all things to all men so that by all possible means I might save some. I do all this for the sake of the gospel, that I may share in its blessings.*
>
> *—1 Corinthians 9:16-23*

asked why. He said to me, "God can save Muslims without your help, Fouad."

Looking back, this story makes me chuckle. Of course God doesn't need my help. I know that God is able to move on the hearts of every Muslim worldwide and save them all while I sit and drink my coffee. In fact, I've heard countless true stories in which He has sent dreams, visions, angels, and signs to Muslims as His method for bringing those individuals into His kingdom. God even used the fear of one American-born Iranian Muslim I met. After September 11, 2001, he was afraid that the Christians would kill all the Muslims, so he bought a New Testament to see if its teachings confirmed his fears. By October he had placed his faith in Christ, joined an Iranian Christian fellowship, and been baptized.

To go is both obedience and faith; to refuse is both disobedience and disbelief.

God can use any method He wants!

But here is the essence of what I told my skeptical friend: From the beginning, Jesus chose mere people to be His messengers. He didn't command us to *watch* while He made disciples of all nations. He commanded us to *go*. And as we're going, He commanded us to *make disciples*. And as we go and make disciples, we—mere people—do so by the authority of Jesus Christ, rightful claimant to all authority in heaven and on earth.

God's absolute sovereignty does not excuse us from the Great Commission—rather, it empowers our going. We go, not because God needs us to, but because the incarnate Word of God, the Messiah, the risen Lord of all has told us to. And our going is effective because He who sits on the throne, possessor of all authority, has promised, "Surely I am with you always, to the very end of the age" (Matthew 28:20).

To go is both obedience and faith; to refuse is both disobedience and disbelief.

Conquering Our Culture of Apathy

If Christ has all authority in heaven and earth—and He does—we have no excuse for disengaging from His parting mandate. From the beginning He has commanded that mere people must be His vehicles of the good news—*effective* vehicles because we are accompanied by His presence and power.

What then shall we do about the church's culture of apathy? In my estimation, apathy is worse than racism. Racist people are at least acting on their beliefs. The heart of a racist can be redirected; he can repent and turn his energies from racism toward good. But only with great effort can the apathetic be jolted from their lethargy. In the apt words of Pink Floyd, they've become "comfortably numb."[9] Toward Muslims and other groups of lost people, such Christians feel nothing. They may voice an opinion, but their inaction reveals a total absence of heartfelt concern.

Our apathy has left us paralyzed toward Muslims—unavailable for the task, unwilling to stand for Christ, unmoved by the state of the Muslim world.

Yet with Jesus, there is hope for the comfortably numb. Jesus picked twelve disciples who—to put it kindly—were not the sharpest tools in the shed. Their lives were not morally spotless, but they were transformed by Christ. Even after they had

forsaken their teacher in His moment of greatest need, God still chose to use them. Though they were not well-equipped, Jesus empowered them with the Holy Spirit. In fact, Jesus said that those who believe Him will do greater works than He did (see John 14:12).

If Jesus chose twelve such men as the foundation for His worldwide mission, certainly He can use us. Our passion has atrophied from disuse, but it is not past reclaiming. A good Occupational Therapist can rebuild our heart muscles back to full caring capacity. Fortunately, He is on hand and ready to help us recuperate. We can help advance our restoration by means of three passion-building exercises.

First, we can *open our hearts to be moved by compassion.* Apathy happens when we ignore the need. So try opening your eyes, ears, and heart to some of the pain in the world. Make a conscious, purposeful effort to learn about the lost. Visit the websites of mission sending agencies. Subscribe to and read their prayer letters. And best of all, befriend a few Muslims and learn to know their hearts.

Daily people are dying without Jesus as Savior. Millions of Muslims do not know the spiritual wealth we have in Christ. They do not know the freedom that comes from loving your enemies and forgiving those who persecute you. They have not yet discovered Jesus as the risen Lord—much more than a prophet of God. Muslims do not possess assurance of heaven, forgiveness of sin and power in the Holy Spirit.

We serve a God of unfailing mercies and compassion, and He often exercises His mercy and love through us, His followers. In Ezekiel 3:17-21 and 33:1-9 we are commanded to warn others of the consequences of their sin. Once we've done so, their response becomes their responsibility. But if we don't warn those in danger, we in the community of God are accountable when a sinner dies without having heard the good news. Can we claim to be children of God, yet be unmoved by the lost state of the Muslim world?

Cultivating a heart of compassion is risky. It makes us vulnerable to the pain of others. But God provides the strength and courage to bear the burden, and He rewards our compassionate action with joy and peace, along with the gratitude and eternal fellowship of those whose lives we've touched. Open yourself up to the need and you'll find yourself seeing Muslims through new eyes.

The second way to rehabilitate our passion is to *exercise our voice*. Fear and intimidation can paralyze us. We don't want to be seen as Jesus Freaks, so we don't make a stir. But we, the church of Jesus, are supposed to take a stand for justice and mercy, to be known for Christlike attitudes and actions. How many Christians took a public stand against the recent murder of two Muslim sisters in Irving, Texas? The teenage girls were killed in the back of their father's taxi cab for not wearing the *hijab*, and their father—the primary suspect—remains at large.

We must speak out on behalf of those of *any* faith who are being oppressed or persecuted. Like our brother Abdul Rahman, an Afghan Christian who fled to Italy after escaping a death sentence in his home country. We individually and our churches corporately ought to be petitioning governments and praying fervently for right to be done. How many of these governments know that Christians stand against such injustice?

Speak up. Start by expressing concern for Muslims to God in prayer, and to other believers. Be infectious. Let your concern for Muslims help others awaken and rehabilitate their passion. Voice your compassion by writing letters and sharing on talk radio. This doesn't mean you're defending Islam; rather, you're showing that you care about individual Muslims. If you make a habit of voicing your concern, then when you converse with a Muslim, he or she will see your heart of compassion, and you'll receive gratitude and trust.

Jesus said, "What I tell you in the dark, speak in the daylight; what is whispered in your ear, proclaim from the roofs" (Matthew 10:27). If obeying this commandment makes you a "Jesus Freak," so be it. But we must not lose our witness among Muslims; our words should reflect well on the reputation of Christ the Compassionate, showing us to be true children of our Father. You've probably seen Muslims praying right in the middle of an airport, or on the grassy quad on campus. Muslims have no problem expressing their religion outwardly. Let us not be ashamed of Christ and His teachings. Share the good news!

Finally, our third passion-building exercise is to *seek training*. Churches today rely on "experts" for information about Islam and Muslims, rather than equipping their own members to interact with Muslims. Let me make something very clear: You do not need a PhD in Islam to witness to a Muslim. God can use you to be an ambassador, to shine with the light you have in you. You only need to be able to share about knowing and walking with Jesus! This book will provide you with the basic understanding and the few key concepts, questions, and statements that you need.

When a person testifies in court, he or she is simply asked to share what he or she has seen or otherwise experienced. If you learn a few basic principles about sharing with Muslims, the rest of your responsibility is simply to tell your story, your testimony, what God has done in your life. This personal approach will speak volumes to your friend and be much more effective than passing him or her off to an "expert." In the very next chapter you'll begin to gain the simple training that you need. In fact, what you've already read up to this point makes you better equipped than most Christians to understand and reach Muslims.

The World Next Door

The church is in crisis. A theological crisis has resulted from our lack of faith, and a missiological crisis has been the outcome of our apathy. We haven't sought to understand Muslims and we are not going to them. What will it take to bring renewed courage and trust in God to save millions of Muslims through us? When will we overcome apathy and fear by sincere compassion and concern for Muslims who are dying without a savior?

And why does this crisis pertain to the church? It is the church's crisis, because Jesus made the Great Commission the church's responsibility.

Yet even when the church has refused to go, or missionaries have gone with little effectiveness, our patient God has not given up on us. Instead, He has partially accommodated our crisis by bringing the Muslim world to us. Seven million Muslims now live in North America and twenty million in the United Kingdom. Out of the 100,000 Muslims in

Orlando, Florida, more than 25,000 are from one country—Morocco. Want to reach Moroccan Muslims without flying to North Africa? No problem. Pay a visit to Orlando. You can even combine it with a trip to Disney World.

People from every Muslim country have moved to North America. I've never been to Gambia or Kyrgyzstan, but I can have conversations here with people from both places. (Even if I can't pronounce their country's name.)

So, many of our excuses are invalid. Our short-term team members are frequently asked, "Is it safe to go to the Muslim world?" After 9/11, the mission trips that were most often cancelled were to Muslim countries—the places that needed Christian testimony most. But safety around the globe is no longer the issue: Muslims have come to us; we only have to cross the street to meet them.

Several years ago my wife leveled with me. She said, "Fouad, we're falling into the American Trap. We're becoming people who disappear into their garages." Her point was clear: We had become so absorbed in our own life—especially work and church activities—that we had ignored our neighbors. So our family decided together to put a leash on our basset hound, Sadie (whose waddle makes us think she is more pig than dog), and walk around the neighborhood.

You wouldn't believe how many people we met while out waddling Sadie. Two doors down we encountered a Filipino woman watering her lawn. She introduced us to her Jamaican husband, we exchanged some small talk, and we waddled on. Across the street lived a Nigerian couple. Around the corner from them I met a Lebanese couple. It turns out the wife had grown up down the street from me on the west side of Beirut! Now she was again my neighbor, halfway around the globe.

The world was living in our little subdivision, and we hadn't known it. Going forth to the nations was as easy as taking a stroll and saying, "Hello, my name is..."

Who is my neighbor? Jesus shared the parable of the good Samaritan in order to show the young, self-justifying man that all people—both

Jews and Gentiles, including Muslims—are deserving of our compassion, of our neighborliness, and of our extra-mile efforts to address their needs. You already know this? Okay, but when we ask, "Who is my neighbor?" in a different sense—What are her pastimes? How old are his kids? What keeps them awake at night?—sadly, most of us don't have an answer.

A Christian woman named Rachel told me her story. She moved to a new neighborhood and decided she wouldn't wait for her neighbors to welcome her; she would welcome *herself* to the neighborhood by meeting her neighbors. One door she knocked on was opened by a friendly woman with an accent. After introductions, Rachel found herself invited in by the Egyptian Muslim woman, Leila, and Leila's daughter. They laughed, shared stories, and exchanged details about their families. Then Leila paused. She looked at Rachel and said, "We are honored to have you as our guest. You are the first neighbor to visit our home, and we have lived here six years."

Six years! Can you believe it? For Rachel, it was second nature to meet her new neighbors. Our family needed prodding from my dear wife. What will it take for you to start a friendship with just one Muslim?

Just Like Us

We may be seeing the beginning of an awakening in the church to the needs among the Muslims. And I rejoice. But long before Muslims crossed our minds, they were on the heart of God. Long before we opened our eyes and got a clue, God loved and treasured them.

I like the way Chuck Colson put it in his column, "They Want Jesus Instead." After discussing the mass growth of the church among some Muslim groups, he writes, "How thrilling to learn that so many Muslims have been set free from the chains of their sins—just as you and I have—by the power of Christ's blood!" I'm especially struck by Colson's phrase, "just as you and I have." It's so biblical. We were once no different from any Muslim today. Just as Muslims are dead in their trespasses, so we were dead in ours. Just as Muslims are hopeless without Christ, who alone can make them alive, we were also hopeless without Christ (see Colossians

2:13). We have more in common with Muslims than one might think. We both start out in the same state before God: as sinners. And each of us has the opportunity to be redeemed by Christ.

If only more of us had the heart of one not-very-famous woman who made a tremendous impact in one corner of the Muslim World. In 1912, a mission agency sent a young lady named Nellie to the Middle East. After Nellie had spent several years in Lebanon, her agency decided that her small ministry to Muslim women wasn't proving very effective. She had only led eight women to the Lord. When war broke out, it was the last straw. The agency asked Nellie to come home and leave her fledgling ministry.

Nellie politely refused. She was determined to stay despite the low number of baptisms and the little other "fruit." And today, because of this one woman's steadfastness in ministry, her few female converts has grown from one church to thirteen church plants, a Bible school, and a thriving radio ministry.

What might any one of us—let alone an entire local church—with this kind of faith and determination, accomplish by sharing the love and truth of God here in our own neighborhoods?

In Attitude

Our heavenly Father, don't let me fall into the trap of ignoring my neighbors, those living right around me. Give me a clear testimony that I'm excited about and want to shout from the rooftops. Grant me a compassionate heart that is moved by the hurting, as well as wisdom to know how to help. Guide me, open my ears to Your calling, and show me the steps to take action on it. I ask this for the sake of Jesus.

Chapter Five

What Is an Ambassador?

"Should Christians Convert Muslims?"

I groaned as I read the title of the article in *Time* magazine. It angered and offended me.

But this and similar questions have become tiringly familiar to me. Certain reporters and others hostile to our ministry love to ask, "What gives you the right to convert Muslims to Christianity?" The question is rhetorical, clearly implying that we Christians have no such right. And time after time I confuse my critics…by agreeing with them. I turn their argument on its head and explain that I have no business converting anyone. I can do nothing more than show Muslims the love of Christ. The "converting"—the actual change of heart—is a matter between the individual and God.

Critics aren't the only ones confused about our role as Christ's ambassadors. Many Christians need clarification as to what an ambassador does and does not do. So let me clarify a couple of points in the ambassador's job description.

On the one hand, we represent Jesus. Our relationship with Him defines our very identity. That means you and I, the Christian community—in our work, our play, our homes, our communities—in every respect of our daily exposure to people, we represent Jesus. The subject of our message is Jesus; we are always pointing to our leader, the one and only Messiah. In our thought and speech we should focus on His life, His teachings, His death, His resurrection, His glory, His mandate. Other issues may come up, but everything orbits back to our center—Jesus.

On the other hand, we *do not* make people Christians. Think about it for a moment: An ambassador has a distinctly different job description from that of a naturalization officer. A naturalization officer has authority to declare a person a citizen of his country. But an ambassador, in contrast, has the job of communicating the thoughts, wishes, interests, and values of his country's leader in a foreign land.

As ambassadors for Christ, we do not make people citizens of God's kingdom. God Himself is at work in Muslims; He is the one who makes someone a citizen of heaven. God is drawing Muslims into His family, and they must decide whether to accept His invitation. Their entrance into the kingdom will depend on their faith response to God's initiative. If we try to shoulder either God's responsibility or the other individual's, we're attempting the impossible.

Christ is the one who has all authority in heaven and earth; you have no authority to "convert" a Muslim. Don't allow a Muslim's response to the gospel deter you from being faithful to your role as an ambassador. A Muslim's response to the gospel does require that he understand the gospel, and that's where you come in. Your role is to clearly explain the gospel and leave the results to God. If the Muslim friend responds to Christ, great. If he or she refuses Christ, that's tragic, but it's their responsibility. Either way, you have been faithful to Christ as His ambassador.

IN ACTION

Set up a book table. On a college campus, give out free Muslim-friendly materials, such as Bibles and the Jesus film. (DVD) (Be sure to make available a multi-language version.) Curious Muslims may want to know why you are hosting the book table, and your honest, friendly answer could initiate a lasting friendship. (For outreach materials, go to ***crescentproject.org/resources.***)

IN ACTION

Frequent Muslim-owned restaurants and businesses. Search for Muslim names in the Yellow Pages or on the Internet to discover the wonderful cultural experiences available nearby. Restaurants with Middle Eastern, Pakistani, Mediterranean, Somali, and often Indian cuisine are likely to have Muslim employees and patrons. If you haven't tried hummus yet, you're in for a treat.

Witnessing is sharing the good news of Christ in the power of the Holy Spirit and leaving the results to God.
—Bill Bright

Christ's Ambassador Overcomes Fear with Faith

For my first Christmas in America, my roommate Amos invited me to spend the holiday with his family in Cleveland, Ohio. I learned more about Americans in those few days than in hours of TV viewing. Amos's family showed me a side of American life far different from that portrayed on the soap operas and *Lifestyles of the Rich and Famous*. Their lifestyle was simple, yet the warmth of their home and their sincere devotion to God felt familiar, as if I were back in Beirut with my own family.

I remember another meaningful experience from that holiday, and it comes with a warning. Never go to Cleveland in December! As a Lebanese, I had never heard of a wind chill factor. But one day, standing by a frozen-over Lake Erie, I became a believer in it. The temperature felt like negative fourteen degrees.

I had never seen so much ice in my life. Amos told me about Native Americans who crossed the lake on foot in the winter. I was incredulous. No way! But Amos assured me that if the ice is thick enough, it will support a person.

Never have I learned a great spiritual lesson at so low a temperature. I contemplated the prospect of walking out onto that frozen lake, and I realized that if the ice was, in reality, too thin, and yet my trust in it was

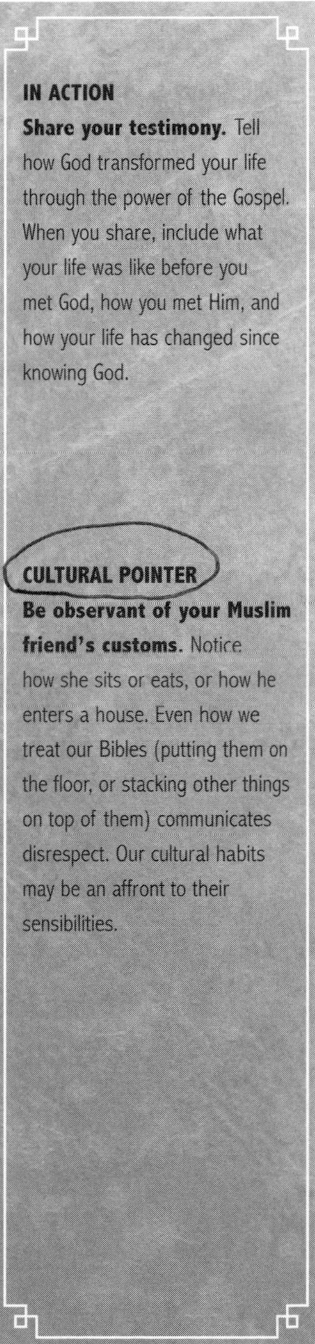

IN ACTION

Share your testimony. Tell how God transformed your life through the power of the Gospel. When you share, include what your life was like before you met God, how you met Him, and how your life has changed since knowing God.

CULTURAL POINTER

Be observant of your Muslim friend's customs. Notice how she sits or eats, or how he enters a house. Even how we treat our Bibles (putting them on the floor, or stacking other things on top of them) communicates disrespect. Our cultural habits may be an affront to their sensibilities.

great, I would still fall through. But if the ice was thick, even if I had little trust in it, it would still hold me.

Our English word "faith" has lost its bite in a culture that deals in phrases like "leap of faith" and "blind faith." Because of this, I sometimes prefer to talk about "trust." That's essentially what faith at its core means—trusting in someone or something. But, as I realized on the Lake Erie shore, faith is only as good as the object in which one places his trust.

Today millions of people are distracted by religion—the many possible complexities of words and activities. But God is looking for those who will simply trust Him. The message of Jesus was to offer people the gift of faith, not another religion. If you have faith in the Rock of Ages, He will not fail you. It's like the frozen lake: It does not matter the amount of faith you have, it is the *object* of your faith. In what or whom have you put your trust?

Fear grips people. Not only do some Christians live in fear, but millions of Muslims are controlled by fear. They are threatened with death if they choose anything but Islam. Government laws, social constraints, and family pressure all contribute to a constant fear of shaming the family or community. Spiritual forces are also at work; some Muslims are tormented by evil spirits.

One of the enemy's favorite tools is fear,

so it's not surprising when opportunities to share truth with a Muslim are accompanied by fear on every side. Some Christians I meet are scared stiff to talk to Muslims. One man told me, "I'm scared to talk to Muslims. They might blow up!" You laugh, but his fear was genuine.

A committed Christian woman I know named Carol followed a *hijab*-covered Muslim woman around a grocery store for forty-five minutes. From the produce section to the pasta aisle to the coolers lined with yogurt. Carol wasn't stalking the lady—she just wanted to meet her. But even standing behind the woman in the checkout line, she still couldn't muster the courage to introduce herself.

When an otherwise fiery woman of God is too intimidated even to say hi, it begs the question: *Is engaging with Muslims really that scary?*

As you continue reading through this book, you'll learn what to do when you meet a Muslim. You will see that when we grasp and hold up the shield of faith—faith in God, the most worthy object of faith in the universe—then we know the "ice" will support us, and fear is destroyed. You don't need to be anxious or fearful about an encounter with a Muslim; you only need mustard-seed-sized faith in God.

Christ's Ambassador Takes Initiative

We've already examined Matthew 28:18-20, but the passage is so central to our cause that we need to take another look. Sometimes verse 18 is left off of Jesus' Great Mandate, so this time pay close attention to the first sentence:

> Then Jesus came to them and said, "All authority in heaven and on earth has been given to me. Therefore go and make disciples of all nations, baptizing them in the name of the Father and of the Son and of the Holy Spirit, and teaching them to obey everything I have commanded you. And surely I am with you always, to the very end of the age."

I can't get past Jesus' first two words: "All authority."

Who has all the authority? Jesus does. Having just defeated death itself, He prepared to ascend to His rightful throne, and He claimed to hold all power in heaven and on earth. Nothing comes as a surprise to Jesus. Nothing catches Him off guard. Everything ultimately obeys His will.

This reminds me how the United States legislature often passes laws that carry implications for local governments. The local government sometimes has to spend extra money in order to carry out the federal mandate. But does the federal law also include an allocation of tax money to reimburse the local body? Sometimes not. Then we have what's called an "unfunded mandate." In other words, the higher authority has commanded the local authority to carry out the law, but hasn't provided the resources to do it.

Jesus' mandate to us, on the other hand, is fully funded. He not only commands us to go and make disciples, but also promises to go personally with us and to provide all authority to carry out His Commission. "His divine power has given us everything we need for life and godliness through our knowledge of him" (2 Peter 1:3). If you were to try to reach others under your own authority, you would be right to be scared. Under your own authority, I would not advise leaving your home, much less witnessing to a Muslim. But when you are sent out by Jesus, you are not going in your own name. Nor are you going in your church's name. You are going in the Name above all names. There's nothing to fear when Jesus is in charge. Under His authority, in His power, you *must* take initiative—you *must* go.

One thing my friend Carol had right, even though she couldn't get up the nerve to say a word, is that she knew she must take the initiative. She knew the Muslim woman in the grocery store wasn't likely to make the first move. Most Muslims assume from the outset that you don't want to talk to them, much less have a friendship with them. They are all too familiar with suspicious looks and curious glances. But a genuine smile? A sincere question? Now that would be something new and unexpected.

I always take the initiative. Even if it's as simple as a smile or a greeting. I ask, "Where are you from?" or "Are you married to an American?"

or "How long have you lived here?" The number one principle is simple: We must take the initiative.

I'm a product of my culture; I've never met a stranger—only people I don't know yet. Cashiers at gas stations and the "sandwich artists" at Subway are easy to get to know. At the grocery store, self-check lines are no fun at all—I don't get to meet the cashier. My wife sometimes gets embarrassed when we're in line at a grocery store or an airport and I start chatting with the guy next to me. She tells me, "In America we don't talk to each other in lines." Maybe you share her sentiment and this is a bit out of your comfort zone, but with a little practice it will start to come more naturally. Do it according to your style; do it your way.

I consider my friend and former board member Donna Thomas an expert when it comes to impacting the "random" people God places in her life. In her book, *First Look, Then Start Talking*, Donna mentions great ideas for conversation starters with people you meet "by chance." She recommends…

- Reading the person's name badge and commenting on the name. This can lead to a discussion about the other's family or home country.
- "Have you been here in this city very long?" You can invite them to share their first impressions upon arrival.
- "What country are you from?" This might open the door for you to follow up with "I'd like to hear more about your country" and invite your new friend to have coffee or a soda with you.
- "What do you do when you're not working here?" is a good one that can give you insight into a person's ambitions and dreams.

Great things happen when you stick out your hand and introduce yourself. A construction worker named Joe stopped by a Lowe's hardware store in Indiana and saw a man wearing a turban. (For the record, most turbaned men aren't Muslim at all—they're Sikhs. But Joe's story is still instructive.) The foreign-looking man was wandering around, lost. Joe had seen him a few times before but had walked past him. This time, the Holy Spirit convicted Joe to approach the man.

"What are you looking for?" Joe asked. "Can I help with something?"

It turns out the man couldn't find a particular sealant that Joe happened to know all about. Joe led him to the right aisle, explained the product and then started asking questions about the man and his family. One conversation in Lowe's led to a cup of coffee together, which is leading to a growing friendship. Thus developed a rich opportunity to witness about God's gift of Jesus—all because Joe offered help instead of ducking behind the Shop-Vac display.

Christ's Ambassador Knows the Starting Point

If you've ever seen the comedy duo Abbott and Costello's "Who's on First" skit, you've seen how two people can use the same words but seem to be speaking two different languages. A Christian and a Muslim come to a conversation with quite different sets of assumptions about each other and their cultures. The same words and concepts—like "God," "good," "devotion" and "freedom"—may be filled with very different meanings in their two minds. You might walk away from such a conversation believing you've communicated clearly with your Muslim friend, when in reality he or she comes away believing you meant something radically different from what you intended.

Part of speaking the same "language" as your Muslim friend is to understand their "starting point"—their current worldview and assumptions about God and themselves, you and your culture. You need to meet them where they are, not where you wish they were in their thinking. If they are going to move toward a relationship with Christ, some of their beliefs about God, themselves and life will need to change drastically, but not overnight. Pray for a heart that accepts and respects their beliefs, but also for patient love that longs to guide them into God's kingdom of light.

Among the beliefs that you first need to recognize and gently try to change are their misconceptions about Christians and Christianity. If you try to explain the good news without first removing these obstacles, your Muslim friend is likely to stay stuck in an attitude of disrespect for all "American Christians," including you.

A young Christian lady was speaking with some Muslim girls she had just met in the United Arab Emirates when the Muslim girls started talking about the glamorous lifestyles of Western movie stars. They asked, "Is divorce okay in Christianity? Brad Pitt divorced Jennifer and now he's with someone new. So is that your belief?"

Most Muslims have never met an authentic follower of Jesus. They assume that whatever they see in the Western media represents typical Christian behavior and standards. Even when Muslims come to the United States or Canada, they are so insulated in their Islamic community that their negative starting stereotype often endures. They do not know what true life in Jesus can look like.

A few years ago I was in Casa Blanca. Although Morocco is "closed" to the gospel, individual Moroccans are open to hearing about Jesus. Many of them would love to read or hear the words of Jesus, the great prophet and healer, but they've never had the chance.

Morocco is a beautiful country with wonderful people, excellent mint tea and delicious *tageene* dishes. However, I noticed something there that was not so beautiful: The number-one movie showing in Casa Blanca was one I hadn't seen, but which I later learned was about an American woman cheating on her husband. This is typical of Hollywood's fare—flaunting such unbiblical values as dishonesty and injustice, flouting integrity and purity. This is the Muslims' window on the West, through which they believe they see genuine Christianity.

On that same trip a man sitting next to me on a train asked if I spoke Arabic, and of course I jumped at the chance to speak "the language of heaven."

He asked, "Where do you live?"

"In the United States of America," I answered.

"America is a bad country," he responded quickly.

Thanks a lot, I thought. "You've been there?"

"No," he said, "but they're illiterate, uneducated, and a bunch of cow herders." (I think he meant to say "cowboys.")

So I asked him, "If you've never been to America, where do you get your information?"

I could've guessed the response: "From television, from movies."

"Sir," I answered, "there are more than 1,200 mosques in America."

He was shocked. In disbelief, he murmured, "Christianity is outlawed in my country. You can be imprisoned for believing that way."

As we've seen, Muslims are not merely uninformed, living in a truth vacuum—they're actively *mis*informed about our faith, taught errors and falsehoods about Christianity. And since most have no means of verifying or refuting what they're taught, they don't know any different. Fortunately, we all have opportunities to enlighten Muslims living right around us, as I was able to do when I was once sharing with a Muslim man. He said, "You Christians worship three gods."

I corrected him politely. "No, sir, we worship only one God."

Twice more he asserted that I worshipped three gods, and finally I could take it no longer. "Excuse me, sir. If you want to teach me Islam, I will listen and respect you. But do not teach me Christianity."

By now you can see why interacting with Muslims is going to take a measure of grace and compassion. Not only must we share truth—we must often first correct the beliefs they hold about us that are simply not true. "But do this with gentleness and respect," as the Bible exhorts us (1 Peter 3:15). For this reason patience, compassion, kindness, empathy—all of these Christlike attitudes must clothe us as we share truth with Muslims. Without love, the truth can feel like an attack. In Chapter 6 we'll lay a foundation of attitudes that are fitting for an ambassador for Christ.

Christ's Ambassadors Know Their Identity

One foundational prerequisite to witnessing to Muslims is often ignored or passed by in our zeal to reach out to Muslims and train others to do the same. It may seem too elementary for us to cover, but in reality its elementary nature means it is too critical *not* to discuss. It's the issue of salvation. Not the Muslim's, but *yours*.

What does it mean to be saved? It means to belong to Jesus in every way. "If anyone would come after me," Jesus said, "he must deny himself and take up his cross daily and follow me" (Luke 9:23). To be saved means to sell out to Jesus, committing yourself in every way to following His commands. An unsaved person cannot bear witness to Christ's redeeming power; you cannot represent a leader you do not follow.

To be saved means to be assured of your destination. You know where you are going. Some claim that such certainty is arrogance. But it's not arrogant to be sure of your salvation when you know you didn't earn it... when you know that it is based solely on the price that Jesus paid and the promises He has made. He says, "I tell you the truth, whoever hears my word and believes him who sent me has eternal life and will not be condemned; he has crossed over from death to life" (John 5:24).

When you are saved, you are also filled with the Holy Spirit of God and given gifts of the Spirit. Just as Jesus breathed on his first disciples and said, "Receive the Holy Spirit" (John 20:22), He still breathes on His followers today, empowering them to live for Him and testify about Him. Assurance of your salvation implies your full, continual acceptance of God's power and resources, along with the willingness to exercise them according to His will every moment of every day.

As an ambassador, you must first ask yourself, *Am I truly following Jesus?* If the answer is yes, you should already see the characteristics of Christ evident in your life, in both large and small ways. You should see yourself inevitably growing into the character of Jesus, as God's child and representative. If, however, you answer yes, but you've been resisting this natural transformation, then you are harboring unhappiness that won't be resolved until you surrender to your Master. He's so good. He wants only the best for you, for His own sake.

An affirmation that you are a genuine Jesus follower goes hand-in-hand with the daily, moment-by-moment decision to be committed to Christ above anything else. As you go out into the world—particularly as you touch the lives of Muslims—above any political or social agenda, you are committed to Christ. Don't let your allegiance be divided or distracted by theological differences with other Christians. You belong to Christ, and your Muslim friend should leave the conversation knowing more about Christ, not a particular church denomination. Many times before a conversation with a Muslim, I will pray to be filled with the Holy Spirit and focused simply and purely on Jesus. My prayer might go something like this: "Lord Jesus, I am ready to share about You. You open and guide the discussion." Through prayer, you align your ambitions with Christ's ambitions, you acknowledge your dependence on Him, and you allow Him to prepare you to share.

This is what it means to be saved, a child of God, a follower of Jesus in this day.

In Attitude

Our heavenly Father, You are my God, my Leader. Take my fear and strengthen my faith to overcome it. Take my timidity and spark me to take initiative. Take my judgment and replace it with patient compassion. Take my indecision and fill me with decisive commitment to let You rule my day—this hour, this minute. May Your kingdom reign in my heart and spill over into the lives of the Muslims You intend to touch through me. I ask this for the sake of Jesus.

Chapter Six

The Ambassador's Attitude

Growing up in Lebanon, I saw various Christian groups come through our city, intent on "reaching Muslims." On one such occasion a group targeted a section of town that had a high Shi'ite Muslim population. They loaded their trucks with boxes of multi-colored fliers and tracts emblazoned with the name of Jesus the Messiah in Arabic (*Isa al-Masih*). Then they drove along the streets throwing fliers out the vehicles' windows. They believed that those who were pre-destined to be saved would pick up a flier and place their trust in Jesus.

Pink, yellow, and green papers fluttered to the ground, littering the pavement, sidewalks, and gutters. Soon the brightly colored fliers became smudged with shoe prints.

Shoe prints on the name of Jesus.

As a local Lebanese believer, I was shocked and offended that these outside Christians weren't willing to work with us. Although their intentions were good, we were the ones left behind to deal with the aftermath—the embarrassment and unclear message left behind by the well-intentioned outsiders. We were the ones left to face the confused local Muslims, who esteemed Jesus the Messiah as a great prophet, and yet saw Christians dishonoring Him by throwing His name into the gutter.

I wish this was an isolated case, but every day overzealous Christians take it upon themselves to throw what I call "gospel grenades" in attempts to win Muslims for the kingdom. Maybe they're not throwing fliers, but they dishonor Christ in the eyes of Muslims through drive-by evangelism that seems inappropriately motivated.

IN ACTION

Invite your friend to a holiday meal. Ask your friends to join you for a family gathering or a weekend retreat with other Christians to celebrate the holidays, like Thanksgiving or Christmas. International students and immigrants will be especially surprised and delighted to celebrate the holiday with you. Share the spiritual significance of the holiday, and your friend will enjoy learning about your culture and religion.

IN ACTION

Give a gift. Gift giving is a great way to start a friendship, a great way to welcome people. This could be any small act of kindness. I recommend giving something practical or perhaps a souvenir of a special nature to show your goodwill to your Muslim friend. Many Muslim cultures follow a system of reciprocity, so expect a gift in return, regardless of the value or type. Say a simple thank you and receive the gift, and you will solidify the friendship.

We want to both honor Christ and effectively reach Muslim friends. So let's think carefully about four attitudes of an ambassador for Christ.

Christ's Ambassador Is Loving

My friend Muhammad was born in the Middle East, but moved to America as a small child. When he was a teenager, he became a fanatic for Islam and wanted to spread the message of Islam and its superiority to people of all other religions. Every Friday he went to the *masjid* (mosque or Islamic center) and prayed and listened to the *khutba*, or Islamic sermon. Two days later, every Sunday, he went to church to debate with the Christians and show them the errors of their ways. Each time, the pastor tried to answer Muhammad's questions and objections with love. Five years later, when Muhammad made a commitment to follow Christ and take Him as his Savior, he was asked why he stepped out to follow Christ. "I could not get over how much they loved me," he said. "I was being so nasty to Christians, yet they were so kind to me."

One intrinsic component of the character of Christ's ambassador is the unconditional love of Jesus—love that blesses when cursed, prays when mistreated. It is love like that the pastor showed, love that responds to a nasty accusation with kind words, that prays earnestly for a nondefensive response and for eyes to see the pain beneath the antagonism. Arguments and debates stop dead in their tracks when faced with compassion. The love of God is stronger than the hatred of men.

This is not the romantic love that Hallmark markets so effectively in the month of February. It's not merely a humanitarian love, where we hold hands and sing "Kum-bay-yah" and go home. No, it is the love that looks someone in the face and says, "I love you no matter what," because Jesus gives the power to love. That doesn't mean we agree with our Muslim friends in all things; it means we accept them where they are, but we love them too much to let them stay there. And we pray earnestly that they will be changed by the life and teachings of Christ.

Islam is devoid of unconditional love. *Allahu Al-Wadud*, which can mean "The Loving" or "The Compassionate," is one of the 104 names for God in the Quran. It has connotations of simple affection or romantic love. It is not the same as the Greek *agape* of the New Testament—the unconditional love displayed in the Bible again and again by God, the one who gave His Beloved for us, His enemies. Most Muslims don't understand the love God has for them—love that gives to the point of sacrifice, reaching even to the worst of sinners. And unless you've been touched by unconditional love, you cannot extend it to others.

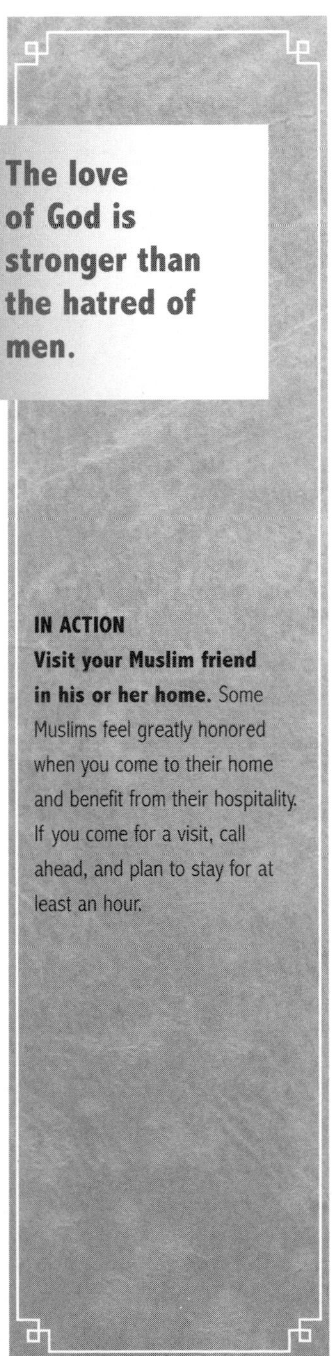

The love of God is stronger than the hatred of men.

IN ACTION

Visit your Muslim friend in his or her home. Some Muslims feel greatly honored when you come to their home and benefit from their hospitality. If you come for a visit, call ahead, and plan to stay for at least an hour.

However, if you are a follower of Christ and have experienced the no-matter-what, I-choose-you-anyway love that Jesus offers, you have the supernatural capacity to extend His compassion and love to Muslims. First John 3:18 explains that love is demonstrated best not merely through words written on a card or promises spoken, but "with actions and in truth." The moment you meet a Muslim, pray: "Lord Jesus, give me power to love him. Let the love of Christ shine through me." *Agape* love is unconditional—it loves, period—and since it was this love that accepted and saved you, you are supernaturally empowered to show it toward Muslims.

Christ's Ambassador Is Friendly

Cultivating a heart of compassion toward Muslims will pave the path for the next natural attitude of an ambassador—friendliness. Unconditional love helps you create an environment conducive to friendship. It doesn't mean you'll be best friends with the next Muslim you pass on the street, but you can take measures to foster an atmosphere where Muslims feel at ease and respected.

The first such measure? *Do not criticize Islam, Muslims, or their prophet Muhammad.* Our role is not to embarrass and put down Muslims, but to respect them and accept them. Christ had harsh words for only one group of people in His lifetime—the hypocrites. Just as Jesus welcomed the likes of Mary Magdalene and Nicodemus, we are commanded to love and welcome all people regardless of race, background, or religious understanding.

When I meet a Muslim, I even go so far as to avoid criticizing his or her country's government. Muslims know their religion and their governments have problems, and sometimes they will point them out themselves. I'm here to represent Christ, to be a friend, not an antagonist. They know Islam doesn't work. They know the Muslim world is a social mess. But they've never heard of a better alternative. You are here to present that alternative.

I can list all of the negative things Muhammad did, but how will that help me build a friendship? It will make Muslims defensive and shut down discussion. My job as an ambassador is to build an environment that's open for discussion.

A man once told me that Muslims need to acknowledge that Muhammad was not God's prophet before they can come to Christ. I disagree. Muslims come to Christ when they see His glory, power, and pure character. As ambassadors of Christ, we must lift Him up and showcase His beauty. Remember, when the sun rises, all the stars disappear. When Christ, the King of kings, the Sun of Righteousness is lifted up, all

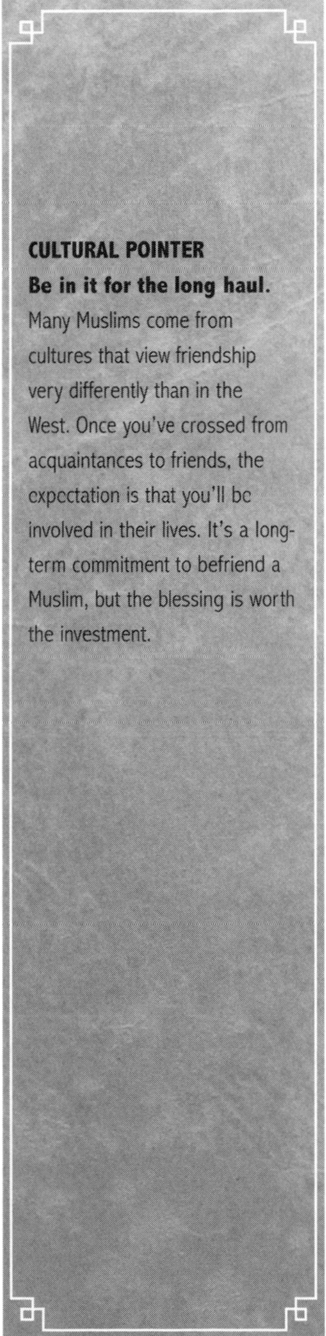

CULTURAL POINTER

Be in it for the long haul.

Many Muslims come from cultures that view friendship very differently than in the West. Once you've crossed from acquaintances to friends, the expectation is that you'll be involved in their lives. It's a long-term commitment to befriend a Muslim, but the blessing is worth the investment.

other rulers and powers—religious and secular—fade in importance.

The second measure for creating a friendly environment: *Don't argue*. We most often argue when we take a disagreement personally; but you're representing Jesus, not yourself. And believe me, if you become defensive and respond to your new Muslim acquaintance with harsh words (even if they are true), he will only remember that you argued. It is far better to lose the argument and win the person. If a conversation gets heated, I will often say, "Maybe I offended you. We can talk about this topic later." We don't have to argue.

The truth we share must be wrapped in love.

Will the gospel bring offense? Of course it will. But don't mistake the offense of the gospel for offense from your verbal attack. Think in terms of welcoming friendship, not competition or hostility. You can respect your friend's opinions, even if you disagree. Endeavor to play a role in this Muslim's learning to follow Jesus. Ask questions. Respond biblically to their questions. And always point to Jesus.

As part of Crescent Project's ministry, we present training seminars on how to share the gospel with Muslims. Well-meaning Christians have often come to my seminars in search of "ammunition" so they can go forth like Rambo Christian and mow down the Muslims. I urge them to manifest the Spirit of Christ. Yes, we want to answer questions and talk about the truth of the Bible. But every bit of truth we share must be wrapped in love.

Third, *friendship requires a time investment*, even if it's a small but consistent connection. A gospel grenade—lobbing the good news from a relational distance and running away—is rarely effective in ministry. Muslims are watching Christians. They're waiting to see if Christians are for real, if we are living our faith, if Christ can really change lives and bring hope. Our time investment, whether big or small, demands that we as ambassadors of Jesus model His teachings. Muslims are watching our behavior. Whether the friendship is a short interaction or a lifelong relationship, they need to see that we're authentic followers of Jesus.

Ask God for grace to be committed for the long haul. That could mean investing time and prayer in your relationships, being bold, not brash, and not shrinking back from the gospel. It means taking every opportunity and walking through the doors God opens. Don't throw a gospel grenade. Instead, be intentional and build a friendly environment in which mutual respect and trust grows strong enough that your friend will listen while you boldly share.

Christ's Ambassador Builds Bridges

The third attitude an ambassador among Muslims should have is a bridge-building approach. The concept of building bridges with Muslims is sometimes misunderstood as a feel-good, "I'm okay, you're okay" idea. Instead, the bridging attitude we're talking about is leveraging similarities—building on commonality—to communicate truth and bring your friend from an old place to a new place spiritually.

Bridging is simple: Take a concept or practice that is similar in two belief systems, and use it to build a bridge. When I say similar, I mean some commonality that is shared by Islam and Christianity. Note also that the commonality is similar, not the same. For instance, piety in Islam and piety in Christianity have similarities, but also have differences. Muslims and Christians both consider prayer part of piety. But pious prayer to a Muslim must include washing one's hands, face, and arms beforehand, and follows a fixed pattern, while Christian prayer is considered pious if it relates personally to God and expresses whatever is on the believer's heart. They are similar, but not the same.

I once was sharing with a computer engineer and noticed he would grow visibly tense when I talked about Jesus being our sacrifice or taking Christ as his Redeemer. So I prayed silently on the spot and shifted the discussion to history and politics. Out of the blue he asked me, "Fouad, aren't you afraid of genies?"

I stopped in my tracks. "What do you mean?"

"Aren't you afraid of genies appearing in the night and choking you to death?" As it turns out, this engineer's grandfather was a village sheikh who was knee-deep in the occult. He would cast spells and chant the Quran to ward off genies (*jinn*) for villagers. (We'll learn more about Muslim beliefs about angels, demons, and *jinn* in the next chapter.)

Here was my chance to build a bridge to the gospel in a way that he could understand. I started from a place of common ground, a similarity between our faiths—one about which my friend was most concerned. He and I both believed in powerful spirit beings—some of them evil.

I also took advantage of another commonality: the prophetic authority of Jesus. "I believe in prophet Jesus," I started. "I pray to Jesus and He will protect me." I shared more about how Jesus is the Word of God (a title found in the Quran, so Muslims agree with it—still more commonality). And since He is the Word of God, Jesus can do whatever God can do. I invited my friend to come under the protection of Christ, the only one who conquered sin, Satan, and death.

Always move beyond common ground.

What started out as a tense discussion ended in an opportunity to create a bridge to the gospel. The Muslim engineer wasn't moved by my talk about Jesus the Redeemer, but Jesus the Protector hit the "bull's eye" of his need.

Always move beyond common ground. You begin with similarities and build a bridge to the gospel. Building a bridge demands moving beyond the commonality and leading your Muslim friend to the truth about Jesus. We'll spend Chapters 8-10 expanding on ways you can use similarities to build a bridge to the gospel for your Muslim friend.

Christ's Ambassador Is Biblical

Remaining biblical is the fourth and arguably most important attitude of an ambassador for Jesus. I always use the *Injeel*, the New Testament, in my interactions with Muslims. Why? Because the Word of God gives life and changes hearts. It does what I can never do.

Memorize a few verses and use it in conversations with your Muslim friend. Because Muslims grow up honoring the recitation of the Quran, when followers of Jesus recite the Word of God, Muslims respect them.

I know a woman who memorized just one verse in Arabic and shared it with an Arabic-speaking Muslim storeowner. Prior to this, the merchant had paid little attention to her, only speaking to her husband to complete each transaction. But one day she asked if she could speak a blessing to him. He shrugged and said, "Sure, why not?" My friend opened her mouth, recited one memorized verse, and left the man speechless. He was taken aback that a woman would have such a powerful message for him. The Word of God speaks for itself, and Muslims often highly regard Scripture spoken from memory.

As I've mentioned, some Muslims will respond that the Bible has been changed or corrupted. When they do, you have a great opportunity to reinforce the authority and reliability of the Bible. We'll get into this in greater detail in Chapter 9.

Most Muslims will gladly accept a Bible as a gift; some will even hug it to their heart or kiss the book. One Christian woman I know gave an *Injeel* to her Muslim sister-in-law as a sendoff gift before a long flight overseas. She wrapped it nicely and included a card that read, "I'm praying for your journey to be peaceful. Here is a gift for

RESOURCES FOR YOU

For a free copy of the *Injeel* (New Testament in Arabic) and other outreach resources, go to ***crescentproject.org/resources.***

you, the *Injeel*, the source of my peace." When the Muslim sister-in-law unwrapped the gift, she jumped up and exclaimed, "The *Injeel*? I didn't know they put it in Arabic!" She hugged her brother's Christian wife and promised to read the book during her flight.

Some Christians are eager to use the Quran in evangelism, leveraging the verses from it that "agree" with the Bible to point to the gospel. I recommend you read the Quran at least once, but I don't recommend you use it with a Muslim. Get a good English translation and read it in order to understand where your Muslim friend is coming from. But using their book in evangelism can be a slippery slope.

You are the Christian. To the Muslim, you are an expert on your book—the Bible—not the Quran. Every Friday he may hear the Quran chanted and discussed, but he is probably not familiar at all with the words of Jesus. Make use of the written Word of God, the Bible. It is powerful and speaks with the authority of the Almighty; it will bring life to your Muslim friend. "My word that goes out from my mouth...will not return to me empty, but will accomplish what I desire and achieve the purpose for which I sent it" (Isaiah 55:11).

I saw the power of the Bible at work in the life of a North African Sunni Muslim named Abdul. He accepted our gift of a New Testament. Nine months later he became a follower of Jesus, and we will all enjoy the great pleasure of Abdul's company throughout eternity.

Our Ambassadorial Example

You can probably understand why gospel grenades rarely work. Here's the other side of the coin: failed friendship evangelism.

I knew a Christian who had been friends with a Muslim girl her age for over a year. "Does your Muslim friend know that you follow Christ?" I asked her.

"Well," the girl said, "we haven't gotten to that yet."

I pushed her further. "Do you want to share with her about Jesus?"

She hesitated. "If I told her now that I'm a Christian, I don't think she would be my friend anymore. I can't risk that."

Many times we falter because we prioritize our friendships over Jesus' mandate to us as His ambassadors. Think about it: In order to avoid the risk of losing our friendship, we hide our faith. In an effort not to "impose our beliefs," we never expose them to Christ. This young lady had established a welcoming environment, but the subject never turned to Jesus and His teachings.

We all know situations when so-called "friendship evangelism" turns into just...friendship. Following Jesus means following His example. But when it comes to reaching Muslims, many Christians miss the methodology of Jesus Christ. "Jesus went through all the towns and villages, teaching in their synagogues, preaching the good news of the kingdom and healing every disease and sickness" (Matthew 9:35). Go through all the villages. Teach. Preach. Heal. That was Jesus.

Christ had a specific strategy. It was *lifestyle evangelism*. He knew that people were both listening to His words and watching His actions. He consistently sowed seeds of the gospel. Using every opportunity and every method to share the message of the kingdom, He purposefully lived to sow widely and reap abundantly. If Jewish leaders challenged Jesus about taxes, Christ used the opportunity to teach, planting spiritual seeds that later were watered, grew, and bore fruit. And He backed up His words with obedient actions, paying His own taxes (see Matthew 17:24–27). In John 4, an entire Samaritan village learned of His life-giving Person, simply because Christ seized the opportunity and asked a stranger for a drink of water.

Following Jesus is always about taking the initiative. It's always about sowing widely—in every part of life (work, school, neighborhood, clubs, shopping) and by every available means (using words, modeling deeds, personifying Christlike attitudes). Too often when Christians practice friendship evangelism with Muslims, days become weeks and weeks become months and months become years, and we never overcome our timidity to bring up the name of Jesus. Lifestyle evangelism, following the pattern of Jesus, helps us avoid both gospel grenades and fruitless friendship by enabling us to sow widely, water deeply, and harvest abundantly.

How to Eat an Elephant

In Lebanon we love idioms and sayings, especially if they are funny. Here's one: "A Lebanese said to his friend, 'I am so hungry I could eat an elephant.' His friend said, 'How can you eat an elephant?' The first man said, 'Bite by bite.'" (I've learned that Americans have a similar saying.)

Reaching millions of Muslims may seem as huge a task as trying to eat an elephant. Indeed it *is* impossible for one person. As much as I love talking to Muslims—the gas station owner, the professor sitting next to me, the exterminator working in my office building—even I can't expect to reach millions.

How can that many Muslims be reached? One by one. Working together, touching one life at a time.

I take comfort in the fact that Christ chose twelve disciples. He saw the helpless masses and carefully sought out people to join the work of the harvest. Jesus determined that the gospel should be conveyed through people. By sharing His earthly mission with others, Jesus demonstrated that the gospel is supposed to be communicated through the words and lives of many individuals, not just one. This simple truth releases me from the burden of believing I have to "go get 'em" on my own; Jesus has ordained that every follower of His will carry His message.

What about evangelism through mass media—via TV, Internet, print, and speaking to crowded stadiums? Is that contrary to what Jesus taught and modeled? After thirty years of working with Muslims, I have found that *no ethical strategy or method should be ruled out*. God is on the move in the Muslim world. Jesus is building His church. Some methods are more effective than others, but a method that might seem weak to us, God can use powerfully to reach the hearts of millions.

Nonetheless, the central *modus operandi* for Christ's ambassadors is the one that He used most often—touching one life at a time with love and truth.

You are an ambassador for Christ, one who represents Jesus in your actions and words. It doesn't matter where you are located—you can be an engineer in Ohio or a financial planner in Idaho or a schoolteacher

in Dubai. In every place, in every life situation, you are an ambassador.

You might be wondering if you have what it takes to be an ambassador. *Am I good enough to represent Christ to Muslims?* If your identity is in Christ, you are His ambassador. God has made you His representative, and that's the only qualification you need.

Lifestyle evangelism is the pattern of Jesus.

Christians are not perfect, but they must be authentic. Be loving and friendly with your Muslim friend. Always point them away from you—the ambassador—and toward your leader, King Jesus.

ᘓ

In Attitude

Our heavenly Father, make me an instrument of Thy peace;
where there is hatred, let me sow love;
where there is injury, pardon;
where there is doubt, faith;
where there is despair, hope;
where there is darkness, light;
and where there is sadness, joy.
I ask this for the sake of Jesus.
—Adapted from a 13th-century prayer by Francis of Assisi

Chapter Seven

Islam: Beliefs and Rituals

I had the privilege once of sitting on an airplane beside a medical doctor who was living in Atlanta, Georgia. By his accent and appearance I suspected he was from the Middle East. I also knew that it was near the end of the month of Ramadan—the month of ritual fasting for Muslims. So I opened the conversation with "*Ramadan Mubarrak*" ("God bless you in this month of Ramadan.") This simple greeting, based on my awareness of common Muslim practice, opened wide the door to further conversation.

My new friend and I spoke of our common origin in the Middle East, and he told me that he was a Muslim. By the time the plane landed, we had spoken at length about Islam and Christianity—particularly about the question of whether God's Word can be changed—and he happily accepted a copy of the book *Is the Injeel Corrupted?*

This chapter will inform you about a few of the most important Islamic beliefs and practices, so you'll have the basic understanding you need to converse with your Muslim friend.

Five Basic Islamic Beliefs

We begin our exploration of Islamic faith and practice by focusing on the *faith* or *belief* of Muslims. In the context of their religion, how do Muslims think?

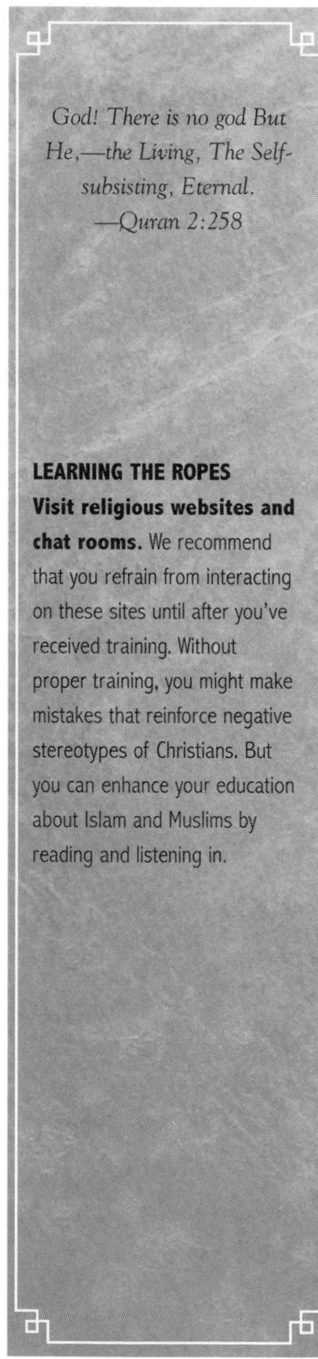

1. One God—Is Allah of the Quran the God of the Bible?

The first and most important of Islamic beliefs is worship of one god (Quran 2:255-258)—specifically, worship of Allah as portrayed in the Quran. The word "Allah" is from a Hebrew root meaning "one god" or "God." And "Allah" is the name used to refer to God by Jews and Christians in Arabic and several other languages.

How do you come to know God in Islam? Muslims tell you, "Know God through His beautiful names." So they like to teach each other the ninety-nine beautiful names of God. In reality, the Quran mentions 104 names for Allah. *Allahu Al-Barry* means "God the creator." *Allahu Al-Qudoos* means "God is holy." *Allahu Al-Raheem* means "God is merciful." *Allahu Al-Malek*, "God the sovereign King." We Christians like a lot of these names because they agree with what the Bible teaches about God.

However, some of the names disagree with the Bible. One, *Allahu Al-Mumeet*, means "God is the source of death." We believe that God is the giver of life, and that death entered the world because of sin (see Romans 5:12–21). Another, *Allahu Al-Muntaqem*, means "the avenger." When you study the verse where this name is used in the Quran, you find that the Quran and the teaching of Muhammad are saying that God comes after you in vengeance, rather than justice. The Quran goes so far as to say that God loves only the Muslims and no one else. But that contradicts the Bible's teaching that God loves everyone, even though we have all sinned and fallen short.

A third troublesome name for Allah is *Allahu Al-Macker*. Quran 3:54 and 8:30 say, "Do not scheme against God because God is the best schemer" (my paraphrase). He can follow His whim, rather than His promise. So when you ask a good Muslim, "Are you going to heaven?" he replies, "I hope so, if God wills." Because in Islam you can be the best Muslim and still miss out on heaven, because God can change His mind.

The implication of these names is that God cannot be trusted. He can be both evil and good. Most Muslims worry about their eternal destiny and use the rituals of Islam, hopefully, to protect themselves from the wrath of God. This is totally different from a biblical understanding of God, which portrays Him as heavenly Father, as the giver of good things, the giver of life, the maker and keeper of promises, the one who brings good even out of evil.

Muslims believe that their understanding of God is the original truth—that the Allah of the Quran is the true God—and that we Christians have changed the teachings of the Bible to come up with a false picture of God.

Muslims also believe that Christianity and Islam worship different numbers of gods—three for us, one for them. But in

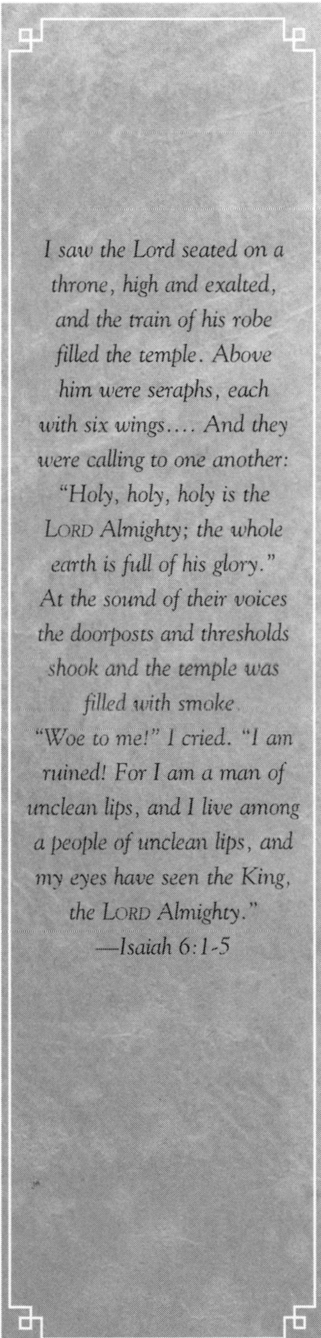

I saw the Lord seated on a throne, high and exalted, and the train of his robe filled the temple. Above him were seraphs, each with six wings.... And they were calling to one another: "Holy, holy, holy is the Lord Almighty; the whole earth is full of his glory." At the sound of their voices the doorposts and thresholds shook and the temple was filled with smoke. "Woe to me!" I cried. "I am ruined! For I am a man of unclean lips, and I live among a people of unclean lips, and my eyes have seen the King, the Lord Almighty."

—Isaiah 6:1-5

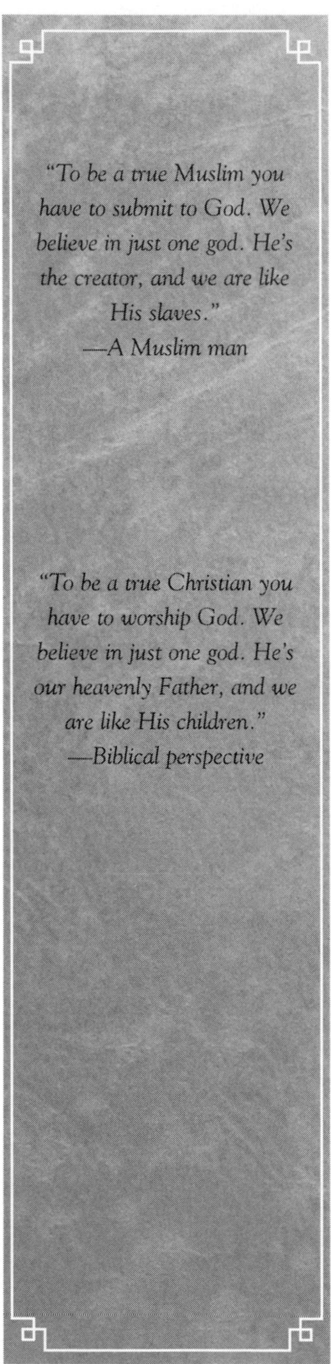

reality we agree on this issue—we both worship one god. Nor do we have a serious problem with calling God "Allah"; Christians in some languages have for centuries used the word "Allah" to refer to the one true God. When I'm talking to a Muslim in Arabic, I use "Allah." If I'm talking to him in English, I use "God." If he says he insists on "Allah," I say, "Fine. Let's talk about Allah. Who is Allah?" And I lead him to understand Allah in the Bible, not Allah in the Quran.

Where the Bible and Islam differ is in the character of God. Several of those qualities of Allah in Islam contradict those of God in the Bible.

2. Angels, Demons, and Jinn—What Is the Nature of Spirit Beings

A second basic teaching of Islam is that angels exist, including demons and *jinn*. Muslims believe that angels are created from light and demons are created from fire. The Quran mentions forty different types of *jinn*, or genies, which are half-human, half-demon and tend to be regarded as controlled by Satan.

Most Muslims fear the *jinn*. Once I was visiting a restaurant, and while I was talking to the Syrian owner, he asked a waiter where one of his other employees was.

The waiter said, "He's in the back doing a *wasfeh*." A *wasfeh* is an incantation to ward off *jinn*.

I said to the owner, "Are you having a

jinn problem in the restaurant?"

"No, it's nothing, nothing."

I said, "If you like, I can pray in the name of Jesus, and God will bless your store."

He looked me in the eye and pleaded, "Please, whatever you do, don't pray here."

"It's okay, I'm going to walk across the street and pray for your restaurant." And I did. I don't believe in *jinn*, but I believe in angels and demons, and I know that demonic activity is real. So I prayed that God would bless his store and cleanse it from any evil spirits. Then I came back and chatted with him a bit.

A year later at another restaurant I happened to encounter the same man with his wife and kids. He remembered me, shook my hand, and asked for a New Testament. Why? Because he saw the spiritual authority that was based on my understanding of the Bible. Jesus has conquered and He has all power and authority to bless us, our businesses, our families…anything in our lives. I don't know if my Syrian friend is reading his Bible or what he thinks of it, but I used our common belief in spirit beings to demonstrate the strength of the God of the Bible.

3. *God's Prophets—Who Speaks for God?*

Third, Muslims believe in God's prophets. Many of the prophets that are mentioned in the Quran are characters from the Bible—especially the Old Testament.

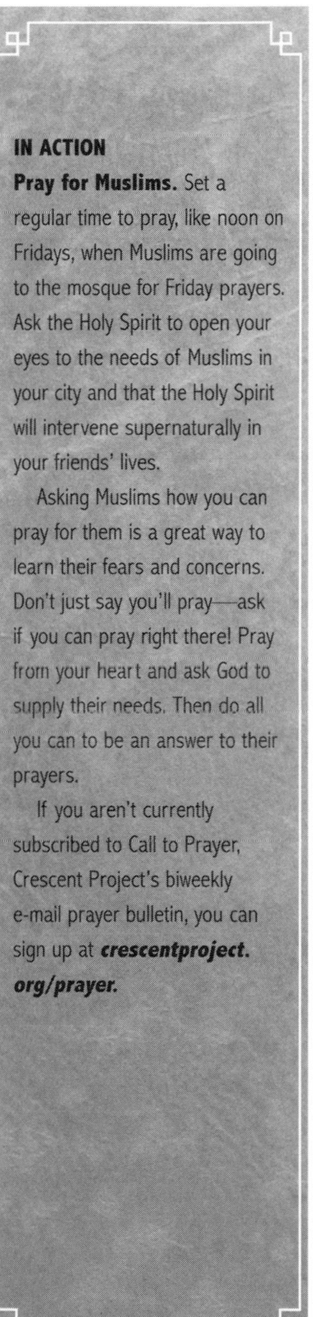

IN ACTION

Pray for Muslims. Set a regular time to pray, like noon on Fridays, when Muslims are going to the mosque for Friday prayers. Ask the Holy Spirit to open your eyes to the needs of Muslims in your city and that the Holy Spirit will intervene supernaturally in your friends' lives.

Asking Muslims how you can pray for them is a great way to learn their fears and concerns. Don't just say you'll pray—ask if you can pray right there! Pray from your heart and ask God to supply their needs. Then do all you can to be an answer to their prayers.

If you aren't currently subscribed to Call to Prayer, Crescent Project's biweekly e-mail prayer bulletin, you can sign up at ***crescentproject.org/prayer.***

> **IN ACTION**
> **Ride the bus together.** If your Muslim friend is new to your area, you can show him or her how to use the public transit system in your city by finding the routes and stop times online. You can also ride the system with him or her the first time.

> **IN ACTION**
> **Attend a thought provoking movie together.** After the movie, have coffee together and discuss your impressions of the film and whether you agreed or disagreed with certain aspects of it. You can emphasize the biblical principles that were portrayed.
>
> In particular, watch the Jesus film together. Afterward, ask your friend if he has questions about what she saw. Maybe a question will come up halfway through. In this case, pause the video and answer it to the best of your knowledge. Point to Scripture when applicable, and show him the exact place in the Gospel where the scene from the movie originates.

The Quran doesn't include the stories and details of their lives, but it does mention them by name. Jonah is mentioned, which opens the door for us to utilize his story to lead Muslim friends to Christ (see Matthew 12:38-41). John the Baptist is mentioned as a prophet, which makes it easy for you to ask your Muslim friend, "If John the Baptist is a prophet, what did he come to do?" The answer—that he came to prepare the way for the Messiah (see John 1:23)—leads the conversation right around to Jesus. Even the Quran says that Jesus was the Messiah of the Jewish people.

The Quran teaches that, among others, Adam, Noah, Moses, Job, Elijah, and Elisha were all prophets. It seems that Islam borrowed significantly from Christianity. And as Islam's prophetic capstone, Orthodox Islam teaches that Muhammad is the *seal*—that is, the last—of the prophets.

Now, some Islamic cults believe that other prophets came after Muhammad. So not every Muslim that you meet believes that Muhammad was the seal. But the Orthodox teaching, followed by the vast majority of Muslims, is that Muhammad was the seal—the last of the prophets.

Bible-believing Christians disagree about the prophetic status of some individuals that the Quran describes as prophets. For example, the Quran says that Alexander the Great was a prophet; we take issue with that. However, in your conversations with

Muslims, don't emphasize our differences. Rather focus here on our similar belief—that God sent the prophets of the Old Testament, as well as John the Baptist and Jesus.

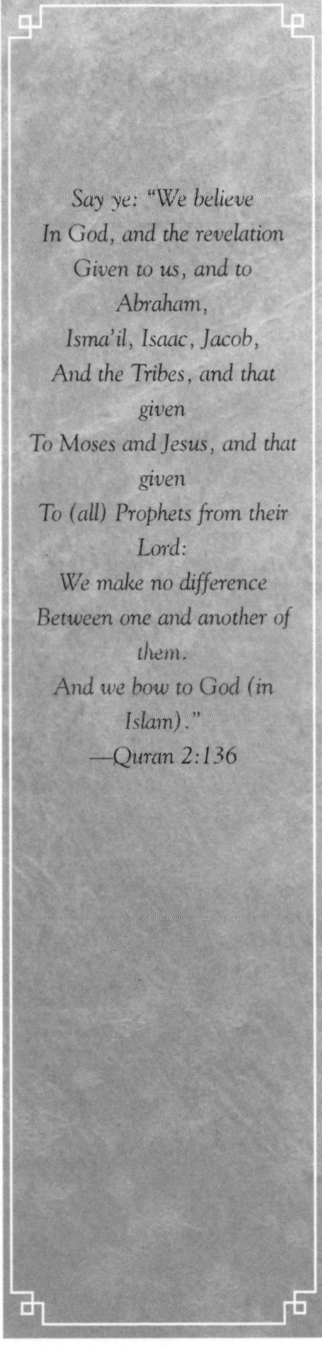

4. God's Messages—Which Can We Trust?

Not only does Islam teach that God sent prophets, but that through them He sent four messages. The person who brings one of God's messages is called a *rasul*, a messenger. So Muhammad and three of the other prophets bear the title *rasul*, a special category of prophet.

What are the four messages that a Muslim must believe in and obey? According to the Quran, the first was the *Tawrat*, the book of Moses; the second was the *Zabur*, the psalms of David; the third was the *Injeel* (literally "the good news"), the book of Jesus (the New Testament); and the fourth was the Quran, the book of Muhammad. The Quran itself even says that God sent the fourth message to confirm the previous three, not to replace them (Quran 3:2-3).

However, Islamic teachers don't seem to agree with the Quran, because they don't teach from the Old or New Testaments. Why don't Islamic teachers teach the *Tawrat* of Moses? Because they believe it was corrupted. That, the *imams* teach, is why Allah sent the *Zabur* of David. But they believe that this also was corrupted, so that Allah sent the *Injeel* of Jesus. This also, the Islamic teachers teach, was corrupted, so Allah sent His fourth and final message, the Quran, the book of Muhammad.

So, you might ask, what if the Quran is changed and corrupted? Islam's answer is, "That's impossible, God protects His word." And there we come to an inconsistency. If God didn't—or couldn't—protect the first three messages, how can we be confident that the Quran will be protected? Or, coming from the other direction, if God is able and willing to protect His last message, why would He allow the first three to be corrupted? If God sent four messages to us, we can either trust them all, or we can trust none of them. By this line of reasoning, you can help your Muslim friend trust and read the Bible.

Besides all this, the Quran itself never says that any part of the Bible has been changed. In fact, Quran 3:2-3 affirms our belief in what God said through Moses, David, and Jesus. So the holy book of Islam endorses the reliability of the Bible.

5. *Judgment Day—How Can We Prepare?*

Finally, Islam teaches that Judgment Day is coming, when everybody will be raised from the dead and will stand before God. Muslim *imams* teach that God is a good business man—that is, you cannot cheat God. Life is a test, and on Judgment Day your good works are put on one side of a scale and your bad works are put on the other. The way the scale tips determines whether you go to heaven or hell.

The Islamic heaven is a physical and sensual paradise with food, drink, and women for the sexual pleasure of men. Hell is a place of eternal fire, where your skin burns off and God creates new skin to burn, over and over again.

Now, what if the scale is equally balanced? What if one's good works exactly balance his bad works? To this, Islam has no answer, leaving Muslims to live in uncertainty and insecurity about their eternal future. Most Muslims are terribly afraid of Judgment Day. Even a good Muslim can end up in hell because, according to Islam, God is sovereign; He can do whatever He wants, and He makes no guarantees to anyone.

What if one person's life contains 99 percent good works, and another's contains 51 percent good works? If they both go to heaven, will they enjoy different levels of heaven? The Quran describes only one paradise.

And how can we measure our good and bad works? How can anyone know when they've done enough good that they can relax?

The Bible says that "if we confess our sins," the God of the Bible is "faithful and just." Faithful and just to do what? To "forgive us our sins and purify us from all unrighteousness" (1 John 1:9). God makes and keeps promises. He is not capricious. He will not change His mind. But we do agree with Islam that a Judgment Day is coming, and that anyone who is unprepared has reason for great fear.

The Five Pillars of Islam

Now we turn from how Muslims think, and we focus on how they behave in a religious context. What are their religious practices? The life of a good Muslim is built upon the five "pillars" of Islam. These are five rituals, some of which are daily, and one of which is expected only once in a person's lifetime.

1. The Islamic Creed—Al-Shahadah

The word *shahadah* means "to testify." This is the creed of Islam, which goes: "There is no God except Allah, and Muhammad is his messenger." Reciting this creed in the presence of a Muslim makes you a Muslim. It implies a commitment to follow the life example and teachings of Muhammad.

The *shahadah* is often treated as a magical statement. In a home you might find it framed in Arab calligraphy and hung on the wall. When a baby is born, the father or grandfather whispers the creed in the baby's ear, making him or her a Muslim. The *shahadah* is recited all the time before and after prayer. It is an important part of the Muslim's daily ritual.

2. Islamic Prayer—Al-Salat

The second pillar or ritual of Islam is called *salat*, the prayer ceremony a Muslim is supposed to perform in the Mosque or alone five times a day.

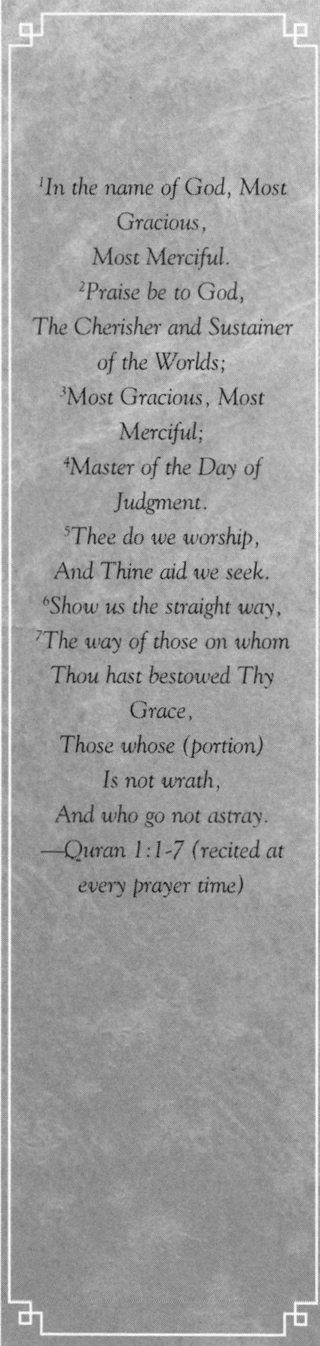

The word *salat* means "to bow down," and it was borrowed from Christian terminology from Syria. The five prayer times are sunrise, noon, afternoon (two hours after the noon hour), sunset, and then night time (two hours after sunset). A Muslim must pray facing Mecca, which means, for those of us who are west of Arabia, facing toward the east, and for those east of Arabia, facing toward the west. Before each prayer, the Muslim must perform ablutions, or ritual washing. Between ablutions and prayer, the Muslim cannot touch a Jew, a Christian, a pagan, or a member of the opposite sex. That would defile them, and they would need to perform the ablutions all over again.

When it's time to pray, the Muslim first stands and recites the first chapter (seven verses) of the Quran. Then they kneel and bow down, their knees, palms, and forehead all touching the ground. Each prayer of the day requires a certain number of kneelings—some four, some three, some two. And since tradition says that Muhammad always added an extra kneeling, Muslims usually add an extra kneeling to each prayer. According to Islam, each person has an angel on the right who keeps track of his good works, and an angel on the left who keeps track of his bad works. The extra kneeling is meant to find its way into the records of the angel on the right.

Now, when a Muslim performs *salat*, Islamic thinking is that it's too much to believe that he or she is really talking to God; God is too busy. But the angels are there tracking one's good and bad works, so one must still perform the ritual in hopes of accumulating more good works. In contrast, the Bible tells us that Christian prayer is a conversation with a personal, present, all-knowing God. We are invited to come and speak to Him anytime, anywhere. He cares, He listens.

3. *The Islamic Month of Fasting—Al-Saum*

The third pillar of Islam is *saum*—that is, fasting during the month of Ramadan. During this lunar month of twenty-eight or twenty-nine days, Muslims are not allowed to eat during daylight hours, but they make up the meals they miss by feasting at night. Islam follows a lunar year that is eleven or twelve days shorter than our year, so the month of Ramadan rotates gradually through the seasons, returning to a particular point on our calendar after about thirty-three years.

The final night of Ramadan is called *Laylat-Al-Qadar*—the Night of Destiny or Power. This is an important night for Muslims, because on this night God might answer your prayers for the upcoming year. Most Muslims like to spend the night chanting the Quran, or listening to it being chanted. Some read it.

If you know someone who is fasting for Ramadan, pray for them on that final night. That's the time of their greatest focus on

God. God often uses that night to grant dreams or visions, or to send someone to talk to a Muslim about Jesus.

4. *Islamic Giving—Al-Zakat*

The fourth pillar or ritual of Islam is *zakat*—giving alms to the needy. The word comes from a Hebrew root meaning "to purify," implying that giving to the needy purifies the rest of your money and earns you credit for good works.

Sunnis give two and a half percent of their annual income, while Shi'ites give five percent of their annual income. Some Muslim cultures today have tried to organize a financial structure for Muslims to pay *zakat*, but in most places *zakat* is not organized. Nonetheless, even without such a structure, many Muslims help the needy spontaneously, as they see the need.

5. *The Islamic Pilgrimage—Al-Hajj*

And finally, the fifth pillar is *hajj*—the highest of all the rituals, the pilgrimage to Mecca and Medina. Every able Muslim is required to make this pilgrimage at least once in his lifetime. Every year, Mecca attracts 1.5 million pilgrims. When they get there, the men will shave their heads and clip their fingernails. Men put on the customary two-piece wool garment and women wear robes. They enter *Masjid al-Haram*, the largest mosque in the world, and they walk around the *Ka'aba*, which houses "the Black Stone," seven times, right to left. As they walk around, they must touch the stone, which is a meteor that fell in Arabia before Islam. The Arabs, who were pagan at the time, thought it was a gift from the god of heaven, so they placed it in the *Ka'aba*. As many pilgrims as possible try to follow Muhammad's example and kiss the stone.

The pilgrimage also involves visiting Medina and other sites, commemorating the events of Muhammad's original journey.

Once a faithful Muslim returns from the pilgrimage, he or she is called *hajji*, meaning one who has accomplished *hajj*. I like to ask these people if they have peace, and the question often opens a significant discussion. One of my friends, who is now a believer in Jesus, went on *hajj* twenty-one times. I asked him why, and he answered, "Every time I went and came back, I had not found peace." His search for inner peace ended only when he found it in Christ.

Why Understand Islamic Rituals?

A good Muslim performs these five rituals of his faith in a lifelong effort to become pleasing to God, storing up good deeds in hopes that they will erase his sins on Judgment Day. Why do we need to learn about the basic beliefs and rituals of Islam? First, because we want to understand our Muslim friends—the aspects of their lives that are most important to them, that shape their worldview and their deepest drives. And second, because every element of Islamic belief and practice that is similar to Christian belief and practice can serve as a starting point for building bridges from Islam to salvation in Christ.

As I said before, you do not need a PhD in Islam to build a friendship with a Muslim. I've given you the most important basics. You can build on this foundation of awareness by connecting with your Muslim friend, asking questions, being a learner. Listen and learn. He is likely to explain something about Islam that you did not know. She might explain an Islamic holiday.

But be ready also for the other half of the conversation between faiths. Your friend might ask you about your beliefs. Prepare with prayer and go. You do not need to become an expert on Islam—you only need to be an expert at being yourself and knowing Jesus.

Types of Muslims

Muslims today can be divided into three major groups. The first group is *cultural Muslims*. They constitute the majority of Muslims worldwide and come from counties where the majority of the country is Muslim, where Islam is the only way of life they know. They were born into Muslim families who decided their faith for them; they've never even considered studying Islam or any other religion in depth. Most of their beliefs are based on traditional information about Islam and about Christianity, and it's easy to talk to them about Jesus. They do not normally adhere to and perform all the rituals.

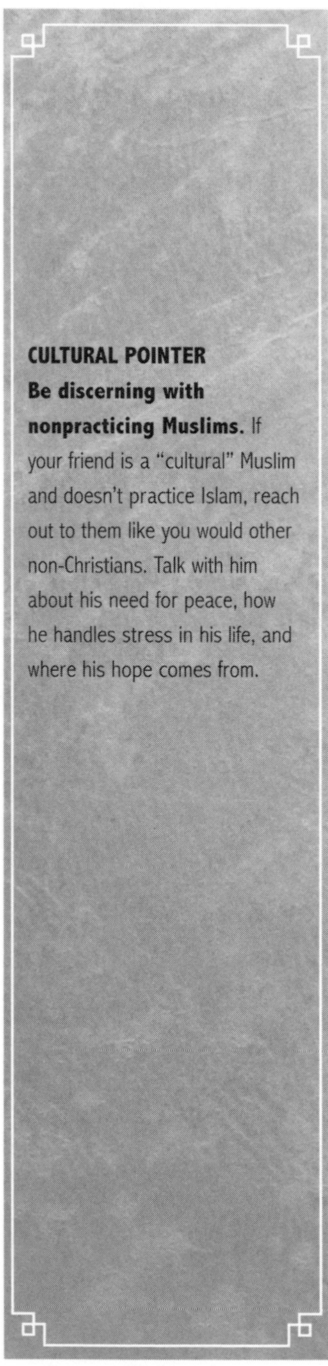

The second group is the *converts*. Converts to Islam come from both western and eastern countries. They're likely to have some religious background—perhaps Hindu or nominal Christian. I like to ask them, "Why did you become a Muslim?" and "What do you like about Islam?" And usually these questions open up a door for us to talk about spiritual things, especially about the gospel of Jesus.

And finally, the *devout* are those who practice their faith "religiously." Sometimes they are educated about their faith, maybe also educated in other academic fields. Out of the pool of the devout arise the militant, many of them uneducated. These Muslims are often referred to as "fundamentalists." Even though many of the devout might tend to argue, try to avoid an argumentative spirit with them. Instead, show love and understanding toward them; let your actions and your words of grace speak for you. Be patient.

One other way to categorize Muslims is by the two major sects of Islam—the *Shi'ites* and the *Sunni*. Muhammad's successors as leaders of Islam were known as *caliphs*. The fourth caliph after Muhammad was his cousin and son-in-law, Ali. During Ali's rule, he fought against a number of different opposition factions, led by, among others, Mu'awiyah, governor of Syria. This civil war (around AD 656) led to the major division of Islam into the *Shi'ites* (literally "partisans") of Ali and the *Sunni*. What started as a political division became a religious division. To this day, the *Shi'ites* follow the religious leadership of Ali's descendants, whereas the *Sunni* follow community tradition.

ഗ

In Attitude

Our heavenly Father, thank You that many Muslims are seeking after You and desire to worship You. I ask that You would bless Muslims with the knowledge of Christ as the redeemer. I pray that, as they are performing the rituals of Islam, they would seek after Christ, who has come to set us free and save us from sin. For as You promised, anyone who commits sin is a slave to sin, but anyone Jesus sets free is free indeed. I pray this for the sake of Jesus.

Chapter Eight

Bridge Building 101

I once spoke with a Sunni engineer from Egypt about life in Egypt, Beirut, and the United States. We began to talk about religion, and he stated that he believed in one God. I told him that I, too, believed in one God, the creator of heaven and earth. We also agreed that God communicates with His people through prophets and messages and miracles. We continued the discussion on the uniqueness of the Bible, and I could tell already that the conversation was going well because of the points on which we agreed.

Often when we talk with people of other religions—such as Hinduism, which believes in many gods—it's difficult to talk about God and Jesus, whereas with Muslims it's very easy because we can begin the conversation with God as creator and God as someone who communicates with His people.

Building on Commonality

Maybe you can begin to see how much we have in common with Muslims. We all agree that we worship one God. We agree that God has spoken through His prophets. We agree that God sent Jesus. There are so many similarities around which we can develop spiritual conversations with our Muslim friends and acquaintances. Notice, once again, the emphasis on *similar*. Islam claims it is a religion like Christianity, but this is incorrect. While many practices and concepts between the two are *similar*, the understanding and practice of these is often vastly different. For example, prayer (*salat*) in Islam is a good work to be performed and recorded by angels who are keeping tally, whereas in the Bible, *salat* is a heavenly Father and His child communicating in relationship.

Yes, the differences are vast. But our role is to build bridges. If we focus on the differences, we'll build walls. But we can build bridges by focusing on the similarities. That's what the rest of this book will teach you—how to take a point of commonality between Christianity and Islam and use it to build a bridge.

To further develop the imagery, picture yourself on one side of a deep chasm; you're in a position of knowing the truth of God's Word. On the other side of the chasm, in a place of misunderstanding and misinformation, is your Muslim friend. The chasm represents the differences between you; it is already wide because of the differences between the Quran and the Bible, and it has been made wider by widespread misunderstandings in the minds of both Christians and Muslims. On your side of the divide, you enjoy forgiveness, a fruitful life, the community of God's family, and hope of eternal joy. Your friend, on the opposite cliff top, walks in a spiritual Sahara, plagued by guilt, uncertainty, and fear.

Your goal is to construct a bridge by which your friend can cross over from misunderstanding to truth, from fear to faith. Your construction materials are laid out on

IN ACTION

Be an English conversation partner. Some libraries and universities have programs to help non-native speakers of English hone their language skills. Why not help tutor an international student, or start your own ESL (English as a Second Language) course in your church or community? Post an advertisement in apartment complexes where Muslim immigrants live or in ethnic stores and restaurants.

IN ACTION

Transport newcomers to appointments and meetings. Taking internationals to doctor's appointments can greatly decrease their anxiety about living in a foreign country.

both sides of the chasm—the teachings of Islam and of Christianity that are similar (though not exactly the same, remember). Using these similarities—along with a consistent supply of love and respect—you can bridge the chasm and help your friend cross over to truth, hope, and faith.

Bridges are a way to use similarities between Christianity and Islam to begin a conversation, which will hopefully lead to a crystal clear conveyance of biblical truth. They help clarify issues and can lead Muslims to an understanding of their need for salvation.

Keep cultivating the friendship, keep asking questions (and listening!), keep answering your friend's questions, and soon you may have the privilege of building the bridge that leads your friend to faith in Christ.

Bridge-Building Etiquette

The most important aspect of building bridges is not the steps of the conversation, but manner in which you conduct yourself. We've already talked about the ambassador's attitudes, and those should be present in you, influencing your words and actions. In review, remember to be *loving* (unconditionally accepting) and *friendly* (establish a welcoming environment). Also be *biblical*—that is, take an English or Arabic New Testament (*Injeel*) with you, or at least have

IN ACTION

Glorify the Son. In the morning, what happens to the stars when the sun comes up? Do the stars go anywhere? No, but as the sun rises and its brightness fills the sky, the stars simply fade away.

The same is true as we lift up Jesus Christ. We don't need to tear down Islam, and speaking negatively of Muhammad won't bring greater openness in discussions. We simply point our friend to Christ. The shining glory of the Son can simply make all other things fade away.

LEARNING THE ROPES

Listen. A good listener focuses on the friend's concerns and needs. Look for bridges between his or her understanding and biblical truths.

several key Bible passages memorized so you can recite them as needed. And, of course, be a *bridge builder*.

In addition, here are a few of the subtle but critically important how-tos to practice every time you talk with a Muslim.

1. *Always start by praying*. Even if all you have is two seconds, silently ask God to bless the other person (He might even use this occasion to change their life) and to open the discussion for you to share the gospel.

2. *Ask for the Holy Spirit to fill your heart and mind*. Jesus promised that the Holy Spirit would give us power to be His witnesses: "You will receive power when the Holy Spirit comes on you; and you will be my witnesses in Jerusalem, and in all Judea and Samaria, and to the ends of the earth" (Acts 1:8). The first sign of a Spirit-filled life is power to live a holy life and to be a witness for Jesus Christ. As you are talking to your Muslim friend, it is Christ and His Holy Spirit who will give you the power to be able to share what God has done in your life with someone who's never known Jesus' teachings.

That's why it is important to pray, not only for the other person and the conversation, but for yourself and the Spirit's working through you. Even if it's brief, take a moment to acknowledge the

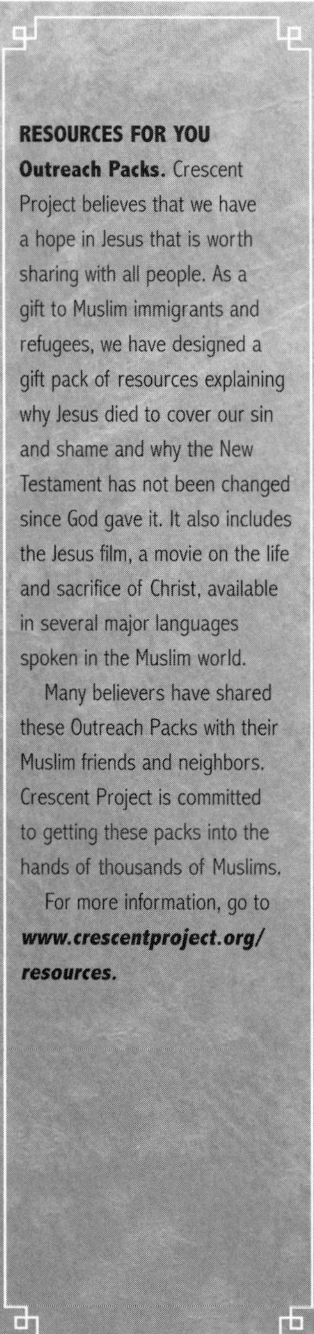

RESOURCES FOR YOU

Outreach Packs. Crescent Project believes that we have a hope in Jesus that is worth sharing with all people. As a gift to Muslim immigrants and refugees, we have designed a gift pack of resources explaining why Jesus died to cover our sin and shame and why the New Testament has not been changed since God gave it. It also includes the Jesus film, a movie on the life and sacrifice of Christ, available in several major languages spoken in the Muslim world.

Many believers have shared these Outreach Packs with their Muslim friends and neighbors. Crescent Project is committed to getting these packs into the hands of thousands of Muslims.

For more information, go to ***www.crescentproject.org/resources.***

Spirit's presence and power, and renew an attitude of dependence and expectation.

I remember sitting next to a gentleman on a flight from Beirut to Istanbul. I turned to him and asked, "What's your name?"

He said, "It's Towfic."

I said, "My name is Fouad."

He was from my home country, Lebanon. As we talked, he secured his seatbelt, and I thought, *Great, he's going nowhere. I'm going to talk about Jesus.* So I prayed, *Lord Jesus, I'm ready to share about You. You open the discussion. You fill me with Your Holy Spirit and show Your power here.*

Towfic looked at me and asked, "What do you do?"

I said, "I'm an ambassador for Jesus."

"What is that?" he asked.

"I've dedicated my life to telling people about Christ," I said. "I've given my life to full-time Christian work."

He wanted to know more, so I shared with him a booklet that explains the way of salvation. When we got to the salvation prayer, he said, "I've been searching to repent of my sins for two years."

"Would you like to repent now?" I asked.

He said, "Yes."

Now, I assumed that he meant he'd pray on his own at some later time. But he asked, "Can I pray right now on the plane?" So he prayed the sinner's prayer, repented of his sins, and accepted Jesus Christ as his Savior.

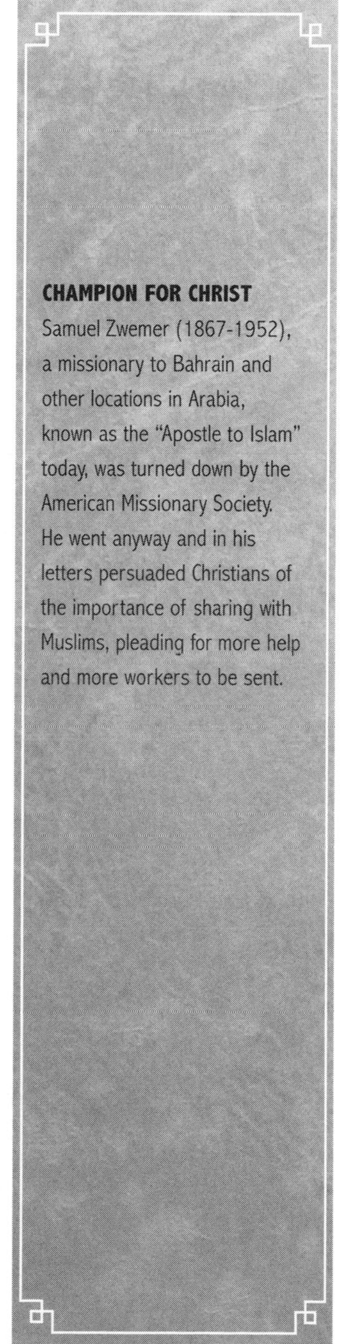

CHAMPION FOR CHRIST

Samuel Zwemer (1867-1952), a missionary to Bahrain and other locations in Arabia, known as the "Apostle to Islam" today, was turned down by the American Missionary Society. He went anyway and in his letters persuaded Christians of the importance of sharing with Muslims, pleading for more help and more workers to be sent.

Here was a man who left Beirut a nonbeliever and landed in Istanbul a believer. That's the joy of praying and following God's plan for the conversation, wherever He chooses it to go.

3. *Gather basic information*. As I did in the preceding story, ask for the other person's name, their country of origin, and any other basics, such as, "What are you doing here?" At the least, this is one way of showing interest in the other person. And you never know how one bit of information might open a door for you to share, or might lead the other person to deeper openness.

4. *Be straightforward*. This is important. You are a believer in Jesus, you are a Christian. Present your faith in a straightforward manner. Muslims are very open to discussing spiritual issues, and Jesus is a famous and highly respected prophet. So don't beat around the bush.

Sometimes Muslims ask me, "Are you Muslim or Christian?"

I might say something like, "I am a follower of Christ," or "I'm a muslim through Jesus." Because the word *muslim* means "one who surrenders." I'm telling them that I have truly surrendered to God through Jesus.

Many times people will say, "Oh, you're a practicing Christian." I simply respond, "Yes, I'm a committed Christian," or "Absolutely, I'm a follower of Christ." Muslims appreciate commitment—you respect them, and they will respect you.

5. *Speak with a smile*. You can say practically anything if you are smiling. Even if you receive criticism, keep smiling. Behind most criticisms you'll find misunderstanding, so try not to become defensive; show compassion because the other person has been misled and misinformed. With gentleness and kindness, answer the criticism in order to correct false information about Christ and Christianity, then move ahead into further respectful, bridge-building conversation.

6. *Do not witness to Muslims in a group*. Because of the shame culture,

Muslims are sometimes afraid to ask questions about other faiths in front of other Muslims. They keep up a front of disinterest. So if I encounter a Muslim in a group and want to talk with him about Christ—even if he initiates with a question—I usually either take him aside, one on one, or I set an appointment to talk at another time. It's very important that your friend trusts you and feels open to talk about spiritual things and asks you questions that he or she cannot ask in front of other Muslims.

7. *Relax, don't panic*. So trust Him. All you have to do to swim on your back is to trust the water to lift you. You relax; you surrender the buoyancy of your body to the water. Likewise, whenever you're witnessing, you surrender and you trust God to give you wisdom in what to say and do. God will use this book and other tools to equip you with knowledge and methods to approach your Muslim friend. However, it is God the Holy Spirit who will guide you as to what to say and what to do as you share the good news.

We are ambassadors for Jesus; we represent Him, not ourselves. We speak in His name, not our own. We share His message, not one that we've come up with. And most significantly, God Almighty lives within you and it's by His power and wisdom that you speak and act. So trust Him.

Which brings us back to our first point: Express and enhance your confidence by bringing everything to God in prayer. Be patient. He will fill you with peace that passes understanding. And, what is more, one of your Muslim friend's greatest needs is for you to pray for them—for their needs, for their family, for their issues. Pray that God will answer their questions about Jesus, about the Bible. Sometime God even works through dreams, so you can pray that He might do this for your friend, if it's His will.

Pray that God will use you in your friend's life. And expect results.

You are here on earth to represent Jesus, day in and day out. God will move in and through you to accomplish His will. So relax, don't panic.

This is God's work and God will receive the glory.

8. *Give a gift*. Gift giving solidifies relationships in a Middle Eastern culture. From the time of Jesus on, gift giving and blessing others has been

a way to show love and respect. I would recommend that you always have something to give to your Muslim friend—something spiritual in nature that focuses on the teachings of Jesus. Perhaps a Bible in his language or a New Testament in both English and Arabic (if he speaks Arabic). Maybe a copy of the book *Is the Injeel Corrupted?* or some other book on Christian thought and devotion. Many Muslims appreciate music; you might offer worship music in English or in the language of her country of origin. If you're always prepared with this type of gift, you'll be continually providing your friend with more that will, in one way or another, draw him closer to Christ.

Case Studies in Building Bridges

The Five Pillars of Christianity

Islam seems to like the number five. As we saw in Chapter 7, Islam teaches five basic teachings, and Muslims practice five "pillars" or rituals. For this reason, I like to share what I call the Five Pillars of Christianity.

You can introduce these by asking your friend, "Did you know that Christians across the face of the earth are unified by five core beliefs?" Then explain to them the Five Pillars of Christianity: Christians believe in...

1. **One God**, holy and gracious

> *Now this is eternal life: that they may know you, the only true God, and Jesus Christ, whom you have sent.*
> (John 17:3)

> *Even if there are so-called gods, whether in heaven or on earth...yet for us there is but one God, the Father, from whom all things came and for whom we live.*
> (1 Corinthians 8:5-6)

2. **One Savior** who redeems all kinds of people

> *For God so loved the world that he gave his one and only Son, that whoever believes in him shall not perish but have*

eternal life. For God did not send his Son into the world to condemn the world, but to save the world through him. (John 3:16-17)

[Grace] has now been revealed through the appearing of our Savior, Christ Jesus, who has destroyed death and has brought life. (2 Timothy 1:10)

3. **One Spirit** who indwells and empowers all believers

...the Spirit of truth. The world cannot accept him, because it neither sees him nor knows him. But you know him, for he lives with you and will be in you. (John 14:17)

You will receive power when the Holy Spirit comes on you. (Acts 1:8)

4. **One message**, the Bible

Jesus went into Galilee, proclaiming the good news of God. "The time has come," he said. "The kingdom of God is near. Repent and believe the good news!" (Mark 1:14-15)

All Scripture is God-breathed and is useful for teaching, rebuking, correcting and training in righteousness, so that the man of God may be thoroughly equipped for every good work. (2 Timothy 3:16-17)

5. **One family**, the church, made up of all who believe in Christ.

To all who received him [Jesus Christ], to those who believed in his name, he gave the right to become children of God. (John 1:12)

There is neither Jew nor Greek, slave nor free, male nor female, for you are all one in Christ Jesus. (Galatians 3:28)

Your Muslim friend is familiar with his or her five pillars, so when you share your five pillars, this structure will make more sense to your friend. And the Five Pillars of Christianity contains at least three clear points of commonality with Islam's basic teachings—both Islam and Christianity teach one God, both teach that Jesus is a prophet from God, and both teach that the Bible is God's message.

Given this number of similarities, you can then go further and use the Five Pillars of Christianity to explain additional realities such as the Trinity (one God, three Persons—Father, Savior/Son, Spirit) and the church, God's family. Since Islam teaches that the Bible is God's message, your friend will listen with respect when you read or recite key Bible passages that clarify these and other Christian truths.

You can use various of these pillars to lead into discussions that touch on needs of your Muslim friend. If they're lonely, God invites them to join His family. If they're plagued by guilt, Jesus died for every kind of sin and offers forgiveness for anything. If they're confused, God's message, the Bible, is pure and satisfying truth. If they live in shame, Christ has taken our shame. If they live in fear, Jesus has the power; He has defeated Satan on the cross.

Do you see how you can use these similarities to build a bridge for your friend that leads to faith, God's truth, and God's family? Time after time I've seen this bridge-building approach open the discussion in a way that is sensitive to the Muslim and makes him or her feel free to share. This approach avoids accusatory wall building and instead builds welcoming bridges.

The God of the Bible

Both Christians and Muslims agree that God is one. This is a great starting point for talking to a Muslim, building bridges right from the get-go. You might explain to your friend one or two of the names or qualities of God that we hold in common, like *Allahu Al-Barry*, the Creator, or *Allahu Al-Raheem*, the Merciful.

The most significant difference to bridge regarding the God of the Bible has to do with the doctrine of the Trinity. The word combines the prefix "tri-" (meaning "three") and "unity" (meaning "oneness"), and was coined in order to describe the Bible's clear teaching of three Persons in one God.

The Muslim's Logic. This Bible teaching is hard enough for Christians to understand, even though we accept it as truth. It's no wonder that people of other faiths become confused about it. In fact, most Muslims, when they hear us speak of the Trinity, are convinced that we are talking about worship of three gods: God, Jesus, and Mary. Islam's strong teaching against idolatry—worshipping any god other than Allah—harkens back to the beginnings of Islam and Muhammad's opposition to the pre-Islamic paganism of the Arabs. Muslims respect the great prophet Jesus, and they know He would never promote idolatry. So, logically, they assume that Christians have departed from the true teachings of Jesus, and that we are the misguided ones. Related Quranic passages: 5:76; 112:1-4; 4:171; 5:119-122; 26:213.

Biblical foundation. In fact, we worship only God. However, as the New Testament teaches, God exists as three Persons. These persons—the Father, the Son, and the Holy Spirit—are not separate Gods, but they are all three equally God. The reason we believe this doctrine, even though it is above our reason, is because the New Testament clearly states it.

Your approach. First, it's important to

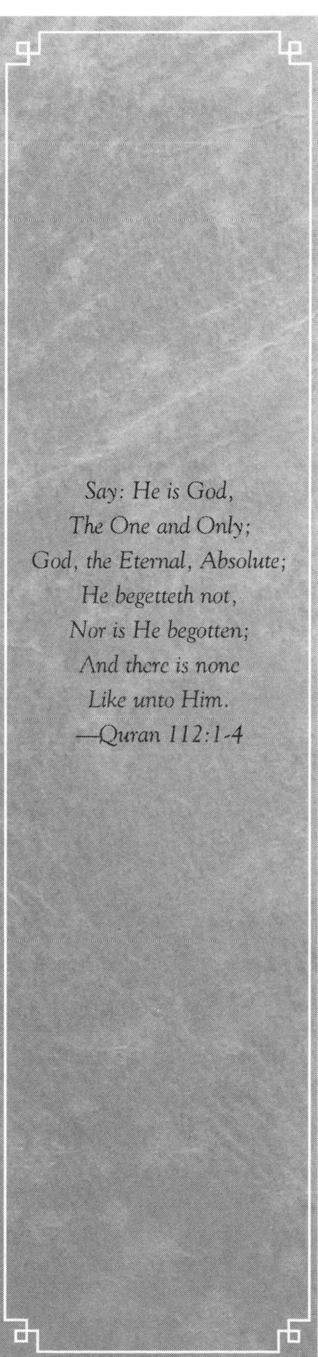

emphasize that the New Testament is your authority, and that it teaches the doctrine of the Trinity. Your Muslim friend understands and respects the authority of God's message, and he or she is likely to respect the *Injeel's* teaching. If he or she objects that the New Testament has been corrupted, you can still proceed with your discussion of the Trinity, but you will also probably need to address the question of the New Testament's integrity at some time (see Chapter 9).

Second, show your friend from the New Testament that the Trinity includes the Father, the Son (also called the Word of God in both the Bible and the Quran), and the Holy Spirit. For example, Matthew 28:18-20 instructs us to baptize believers "in the name of the Father and of the Son and of the Holy Spirit." The word "name" in this passage is singular; we baptize believers into one name for God. The name of God is "the name of the Father and of the Son and of the Holy Spirit"—the three Persons who are one God.

In John 10:30, Jesus claimed quite plainly, "I and the Father are one," and the Jewish leaders wanted to stone Him for blasphemy, because they knew He was claiming to be God (verse 31). In John 5:17, Jesus said, "My Father is always at his work to this very day, and I, too, am working." The Jewish leaders wanted to kill Him because "he was even calling God his own Father, making himself equal with God" (verse 18). And in John 14: 9, Jesus said to His disciples, "Anyone who has seen me has seen the Father."

As for the divinity of the Holy Spirit, 2 Corinthians 3:18 says that the Lord, meaning God, "is the Spirit."

Many other New Testament passages (such as John 14:16-17; 16:13) support the teaching that the Father, the Son, and the Holy Spirit are all three one God, and are somehow also separate Persons.

As you share with your friend, point out that nowhere in the New Testament is Mary said to be a member of the Trinity, and that no Christians believe she is.

Third, explain that even though the Trinity is clearly taught as fact in the Bible, God's nature cannot be completely understood by our limited human minds. A number of illustrations help make sense of God's three-in-one nature, even though none of the illustrations is a perfect analogy. For example, when we add the three Persons of the Trinity (1 + 1 + 1), we get an answer of 3. This is what we humans might expect—three gods. However, the Trinity is more like multiplying: 1 x 1 x 1 = 1 God.

Or you might draw an equilateral triangle (all sides of equal length), the three corners representing the three Persons in one God (one triangle). Another illustration: Water can take three forms—solid (ice), liquid, and gas (steam or water vapor). One substance, three forms.

Another approach is to point out that Jesus is God's Word (John 1:1-4, 14) and the Holy Spirit is God's Spirit (1 Corinthians 12:3; Ephesians 4:30; Romans 8:9, 11). So to believe in the Trinity is to believe in God, His Word, and His Spirit. The Bible teaches that all three Persons of the Trinity are *coeternal*—that is, all three existed since eternity past. Now, for sake of argument, let's suppose this weren't true. Then which existed first? If God existed first, without His Word, then He would have been powerless, because God's Word is His power. If God existed first, without His Spirit, He would be dead. Since God could never exist without power or life, He had to exist eternally with His Word (Jesus) and His Spirit (the Holy Spirit). All three Persons of the Trinity existed together throughout eternity past.

The Jesus of the Bible

One important area of common ground we share with Muslims has to do with respect for Jesus Christ. Although Jesus is mentioned more than ninety-three times in the Quran—roughly four times as many as Muhammad—Muslims lack the biblical understanding of who Jesus is and His role as the promised Messiah. Many verses in the Quran are similar to and sometimes agree with biblical verses, however Jesus in Islam is not described the same way as Jesus in the Bible.

The Quran describes Jesus as one of God's prophets, and yet also unique among the other prophets. The *imams*, on the other hand, don't want to acknowledge the uniqueness of Jesus, so they say, "Jesus was just a good prophet, and the seal of Islam is Muhammad." But the Islamic holy book lifts up Christ above all others as special.

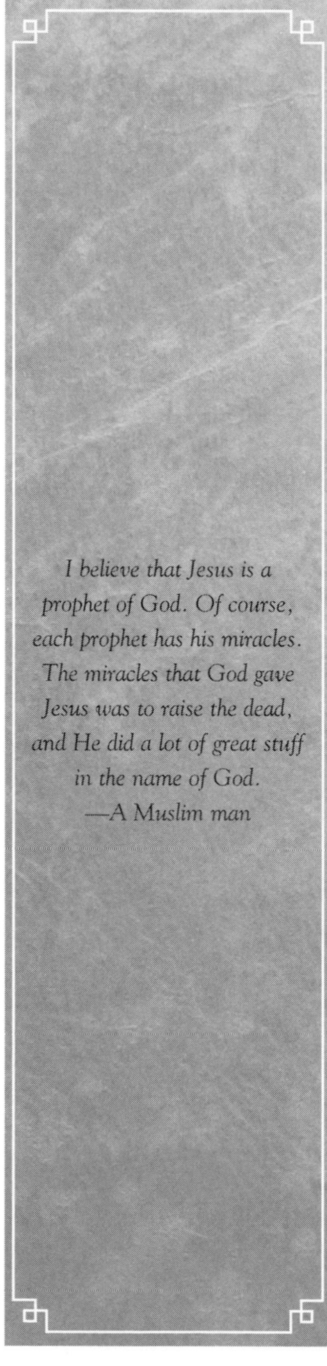

The Quran calls Christ, *Isa bin Maryum*—literally, "Jesus son of Mary." This is an unusual title, since in Middle Eastern culture people are called by their father's name. When you ask Muslims why Jesus is called by His mother's name, they respond that Jesus had no human father, that He was born of a virgin. Most *imams* will tell you, "Oh, we are like you Christians. We worship God, and we know that God did a miracle by sending Christ to be born of a virgin, not like any other human." Muslims believe, as we do, in the one-of-a-kind virgin birth of Jesus.

Islam also teaches that Jesus is the Word of God—*Kalimat Allah*. According to Quran 4:171, "The Messiah, Jesus the son of Mary, is but the apostle of God and His Word, which He cast into Mary and a spirit from Him." Compare this with the Bible, in John 1:1, 14: "In the beginning was the Word, and the Word was with God, and the Word was God.... The Word became flesh and made his dwelling among us. We have seen his glory, the glory of the One and Only, who came from the Father, full of grace and truth."

God's Word is powerful. Both the Quran and the Bible tell how Jesus healed the sick, raised the dead, and performed other types of miracles. Just as God created human life from the dust, the Quran tells a story of Jesus shaping birds from mud, giving them life, and sending them flying off.

The Quran also teaches that Christ will be the Intercessor on Judgment Day. In other words, the human prophet Jesus has been chosen by God, out of all those He might have chosen, to speak to God on behalf of the faithful before God's judgment throne. I don't know how much hope this gives Muslims, but as a Christian, I am grateful that my Savior will be interceding for me before the Divine Judge.

Taken together, these similarities between Christianity and Islamic teaching provide us with many options to begin building bridges for our Muslim friends to cross to the Jesus of the Bible. And that brings us to the differences that we need to bridge over.

The Muslim's logic. While it's true that Muslims and Christians agree on the virgin birth of Jesus, we disagree on the nature of Jesus' divine sonship. Whenever Muslims hear us say that Jesus is the Son of God, they think we are like the pagans, that we believe that God, incarnated in the angel Gabriel, had a sexual relationship with Mary—a blasphemous concept—and that Jesus is therefore half human, half god. This is like the idolatrous Greek theology with their pantheon of gods, like Zeus, who dallied with human women and begat children that were half-gods. You can see how Muslims might lump us together with other pagan religions. Related Quranic passages: 5:17-19; 5:75; 6:100-103; 10:67-68; 112:1-4.

Biblical foundation. God doesn't have to resort to human sexuality; He can do all things. God the Son, who existed eternally with the Father and the Spirit, miraculously took on flesh and became the unique God-man, fully God and fully human. Jesus became the incarnate ("made flesh") Word of God. Jesus is Son to God the Father in a spiritual sense, not a physical sense.

Your approach. First, as with any Christian teaching, emphasize that it is the New Testament, the *Injeel*, that teaches this. You're not making this up yourself; you're sharing from the authority of God's message. (If your friend objects that the *Injeel* has been corrupted, see Chapter 9 about how to support the validity of the Bible.)

Second, ask your friend, "Do we agree that God can do all things?" Of course, every Muslim will agree. Then explain that God can perform any miracle any way He wishes; He was not limited to sexual reproduction in order to conceive His Son within Mary, but performed a miracle in the incarnation of Jesus. God incarnated (made flesh) Jesus, His Word, because He wisely chose to communicate best through His Son in human form.

Another question you might ask is, "Is there a difference between God and His Word? Or are they the same?" Since Islam teaches that God and His Word are the same, most Muslims will answer accordingly. This is a good time, then, to read John 1:1-4, 14, emphasizing that "the Word" in this passage is Jesus (verse 14), who "was God," who "was with God in the beginning" (in eternity past), who created all things, and who is the source of life and light for all men. In other words, Jesus is fully God and has always been. Similar passages are Hebrews 1:1-5 and 1 Timothy 3:16.

Third, stress that Jesus' divine sonship is spiritual, not physical. Jesus is the Son of God the Father in a spiritual sense, not in a physical sense.

Fourth, read or recite additional Bible passages that teach the truth about Jesus' incarnation and nature. As you do this, emphasize that although the Bible teaches these things, they are above human reason. Like the Trinity, they are true, but they are not fully comprehensible to our limited human minds.

The two key passages that tell the story of Jesus' conception are Matthew 1:18-24 and Luke 1:26-56. While sharing the story from Scripture, point out certain revealed insights in these passages:

- God's Holy Spirit (that is, God Himself in the third Person of the Trinity) conceived Jesus in Mary (Matthew 1:18, 20; Luke 1:35), not sexually, but miraculously; not by an angel, but by God's power and will.
- Jesus' name (a variation on "Joshua," meaning "Yahweh is salvation") was foretold because He would be mankind's only means of salvation from sin (Matthew 1:21; Luke 1:31).
- Jesus was called "Immanuel," which is Hebrew for "God with us" (Matthew 1:23).
- The angel Gabriel was only a messenger to Mary (Luke 1:26-38);

he never had any physical relationship with her.

- The New Testament calls Jesus the Son of God (Luke 1:32, 35); this is not a title made up by Christians.
- Jesus fulfilled God's promise to King David of an eternal King (Luke 1:32-33; 2 Samuel 7:12-13, 16); Jesus is far more than a prophet. [Both Mary (Luke 1:27) and Joseph (Matthew 1:1, 6-16) were descendents of David; Mary was the physical mother of Jesus and Joseph was the legal (adoptive) father of Jesus.]
- "Nothing is impossible with God" (Luke 1:37).

If you want to study Quranic passages about Jesus, to understand where Muslims are coming from, we recommend: 5:17-19; 5:72-75; 6:100-103; 10:68; 112:1-4.

A Story of Two Women

I remember the time when I participated in a dinner provided for international students. I shared my testimony, and after dinner I was speaking with a lady from Senegal about God and Jesus and religion. At one point she said, "The reason I don't want to become a Christian is that you believe that Jesus is the Son of God."

I said to her, "And what do you mean by that?"

RESOURCES FOR YOU

See also ***youtube.com/crescentproject*** for more resources.

She said, "You know, that God had a sexual relationship with Mary."

"Excuse me," I replied, "we don't believe that there was any sexual relationship between God and Mary. It was a miracle. We call Him Son of God because God performed the miracle. The Quran calls Him son of Mary because He has no human father."

She said, "That's true."

So I continued, "We want to give glory to God, so we call Jesus the Son of God."

Now that I had affirmed that Jesus' conception was a miracle, the Senegali girl said, "Oh, I believe too that it was a miracle, that Jesus was born of a virgin." Then she looked at me and asked, "How come you guys worship Mary?"

"Excuse me?" I said.

She said, "Yeah, you guys worship God, Jesus, and Mary—the Trinity."

I said, "No, we worship God, His Word, and His Spirit." And I proceeded to explain the Trinity from a biblical perspective.

When I had finished, she said, "I believe in that, too."

While I was sharing with her, the head of the household was distributing English-language Bibles. She asked the Senegali girl whether she would like a New Testament. I was a little surprised when she politely declined, until I realized that an Iranian girl had been standing behind me, listening to our conversation. However, when the Iranian girl reached out and said, "I would like a Bible," the girl from Senegal said, "I would love a copy."

My prayer is that both of these ladies would read the New Testament and they would see that Jesus is the Word of God, and that He would become their Savior.

ꙮ

In Attitude

Our heavenly Father, You are the master engineer. You initiated a bridge to us through Christ. Thank You that Jesus is the bridge to heaven over the great divide. Help me build bridges with Muslims to bring them to faith in Christ. I ask this for the sake of Jesus.

Chapter Nine

Building a Bridge to the Bible

I was once leading eleven Americans on a trip to Beirut, and we went downtown to taste some of the city's famous baklava. As we entered the store, the owner asked me if I was an Evangelical. I answered that, yes, all of us were Evangelicals, and we were in the city to pray that God would bless Beirut.

The store owner said, "Evangelicals are wrong. They follow the *Injeel*, and the *Injeel* has been corrupted."

"God forbid!" I exclaimed. "If all the Christians got together and tried to change the *Injeel*, who would win—God or the Christians?"

He was taken aback and asked me to repeat my question, so I did.

"Of course," he replied, "God would win."

"You're right," I said. "This means that no one can change the *Injeel*. No one is stronger than God, and it is a blasphemy to say that God's Word can be corrupted by humans.

His demeanor changed and he dropped his defensive attitude. "I've never heard anything like this," he said. And we ended up sharing further with him about the history of the *Injeel* and left him with a copy of the book, *Is the Injeel Corrupted?*

Once we get past the barriers of misunderstanding and misperception, Christians and Muslims can have wonderful conversations about God's messages to humanity.

God's Men and Their Messages

As we saw in Chapter 7, one area of commonality between Islam and Christianity is that we both believe in God's prophets. For example,

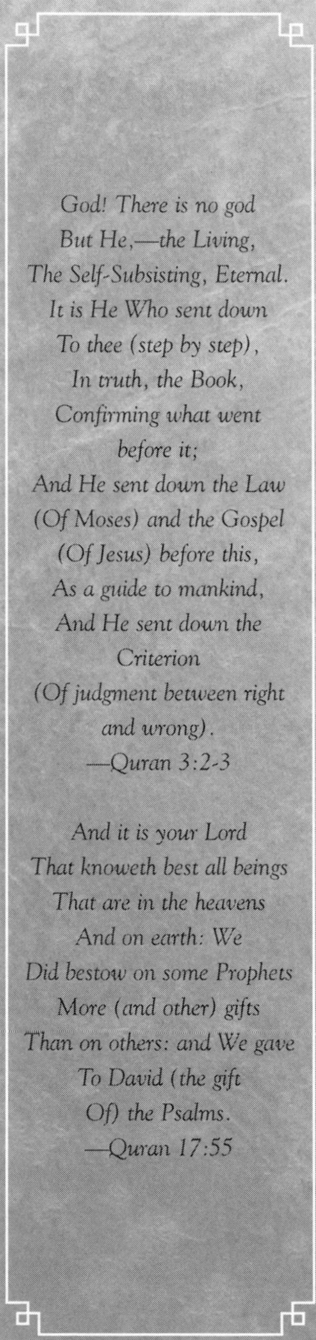

in Islam, Adam is a prophet. We agree that Adam knew about God. Now, can we talk with a Muslim friend about the story of Adam and come back around to Jesus? Absolutely! Christ became the new Adam, He is righteousness in this earth (see Romans 5:12-21).

Or Noah. Can we start with the prophet Noah and come back to Jesus? Absolutely! Noah built the ark to protect people from the wrath of God. Jesus is our ark that protects us on Judgment Day.

How about Abraham? Abraham took his son to sacrifice him and God provided a sheep. They believe in that story, too—that God redeemed the son of Abraham with a sheep. They call the celebration *Adha*, which means "sacrifice."

Or the story of Jonah? Christ used Jonah's three days and nights in the fish's belly as proof that He was the Messiah (Matthew 12:38-41).

Muslims believe that John the Baptist was a prophet. What did John the Baptist come to do? To prepare the way for the Messiah, for Jesus. And, the Quran agrees that Jesus was the Messiah.

Now, we Christians wouldn't refer to all of these men as prophets, but that's a minor point. God can use any of these similarities in Islam—these respected characters of the Bible—to build bridges to salvation in Jesus.

Islam and Christianity also agree that, through His prophets, God sent His messages. And while Christians don't accept the Quran as Scripture, both faiths believe that God sent the *Tawrat* of Moses (Old Testament), the *Zabur* of David (the Psalms), and the *Injeel* of Jesus (New Testament). It's true that the *imams* say these first three messages were corrupted, but when you invite a Muslim to read the Bible, you're not asking them to do anything wrong. The Quran says that Muslims must believe and follow the *Tawrat* of Moses, the *Zabur* of David, and the *Injeel* of Jesus.

Establishing the Authenticity of the Injeel

Now, you and I can see the evidence and immediately believe, *Of course, the Bible is true and uncorrupted*. But keep in mind that you and your Muslim friend have spent your lives growing up in two completely different belief systems, and your friend must take time to process an entirely different way of thinking about himself, his God, his world, his salvation, and his eternity. She must carefully weigh the personal cost of accepting the *Injeel* and its teachings about Jesus.

So we're going to use the rest of this chapter to lay out an approach you can use to build a bridge—lovingly, gently, patiently—from where your friend is now to a new confidence that the *Injeel* is God's uncorrupted, unchanged message to all of us.

IN ACTION [FOR WOMEN]

Be a driving coach. Teaching your Muslim friend to drive and helping her get her license can greatly increase her freedom. It might be a nerve-wracking experience, so help her learn in a deserted area (like a parking lot or a little-used street) and pray to demonstrate patience and love.

Sew, knit, or quilt together. Find simple activities where you can learn and participate together; this can open up long stretches of time for conversation, and with the focus on the activity, the conversation may flow more freely.

IN ACTION [FOR FAMILIES]

Befriend the parents of your children's classmates. By getting to know the parents of Muslim students at your child's school, natural opportunities for friendship abound when you can smile, ask a question about their child, or share a story about your own.

Offer after-school tutoring. Are you skilled in subjects like math or language arts? Tutoring or providing music lessons can be a great way to befriend an entire Muslim family by investing in their child's education.

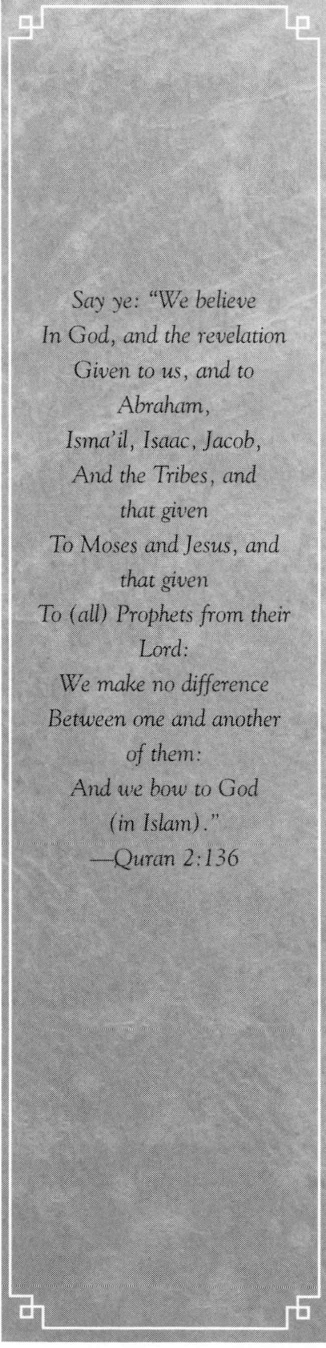

When you use the Bible as your authority for your faith, at some point the majority of Muslims will say to you, "Isn't the *Injeel* corrupted? Haven't you Christians changed the New Testament?" Or they might word it this way: "Wasn't the Quran sent to replace the *Injeel*, to correct the mix-up that your Bible has become?"

Even though Quran 2:136 says that Muslims must believe what God said through the *Tawrat* of Moses, and through the *Injeel* of Jesus, and even though Quran 3:2-3 says the Quran was sent to confirm the message that came before it—namely our Bible—keep in mind that many Muslims today have never read the whole Quran. Maybe they have heard select verses from it chanted, but they have never sat down, read the whole Quran and compared it to the New Testament. The conversational apologetics that we are about to walk through will provide you a way to lift the veil so that Muslims will look at the New Testament and see that it is valid.

We need to learn about the common folk understanding of the *Injeel*. What do the *imams* teach about it? Then we will look at the Christian understanding of the Bible. And finally we will learn how to build a bridge that helps the Muslim cross over from one to the other.

The Muslim's logic. The common teaching is that God sent the *Tawrat* to Moses, and the Jewish people changed it.

Then God sent the *Zabur* to David, and the Jews changed that, also. Then God sent the *Injeel* to Christians, and the Christians changed it to suit their own desires. So then God finally sent the Quran, which is incorruptible.

The *imams* teach that we Christians have taken the New Testament and made many changes over time, creating a series of different versions, so that the original meaning has been lost. They believe that Jesus originally taught about the prophet to come, Muhammad, and the "true" faith of Islam, but that we have changed many of the stories and have deleted all references to Muhammad and all references to Islam. Therefore, the Bible that we have is not true to the words of Jesus; it is unreliable, corrupted with manmade teachings.

Biblical foundation. We believe what the Bible says about itself. For example, 2 Timothy 3:16 says that the *Injeel* is the inspired, or "God-breathed," Word of God. That is, God Himself moved upon the writers and caused them to accurately write about the words and actions of Jesus, as well as the rest of the Bible's content. Christians believe that God sent His Word—the Old and New Testaments of our Bible.

We also believe that God Himself protects and preserves His Word, because He is stronger than anyone else. His purpose in preserving His Word uncorrupted is to enlighten and to judge the human race. He

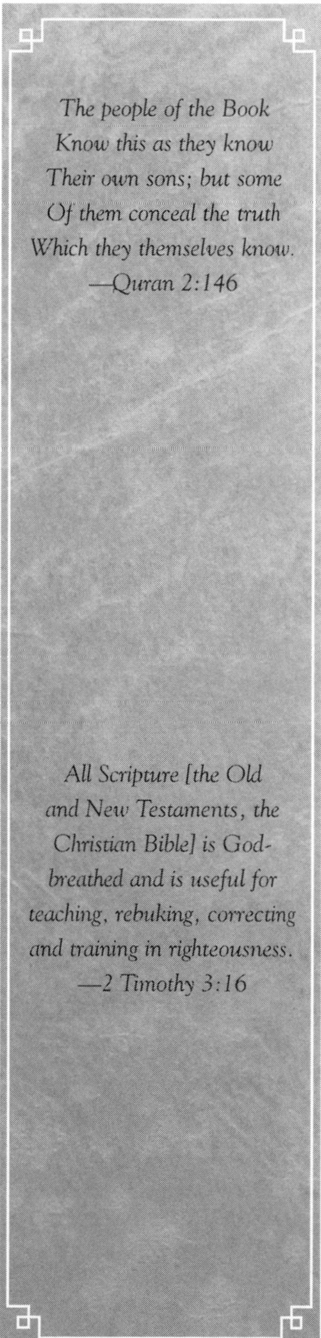

The people of the Book
Know this as they know
Their own sons; but some
Of them conceal the truth
Which they themselves know.
—Quran 2:146

All Scripture [the Old and New Testaments, the Christian Bible] is God-breathed and is useful for teaching, rebuking, correcting and training in righteousness.
—2 Timothy 3:16

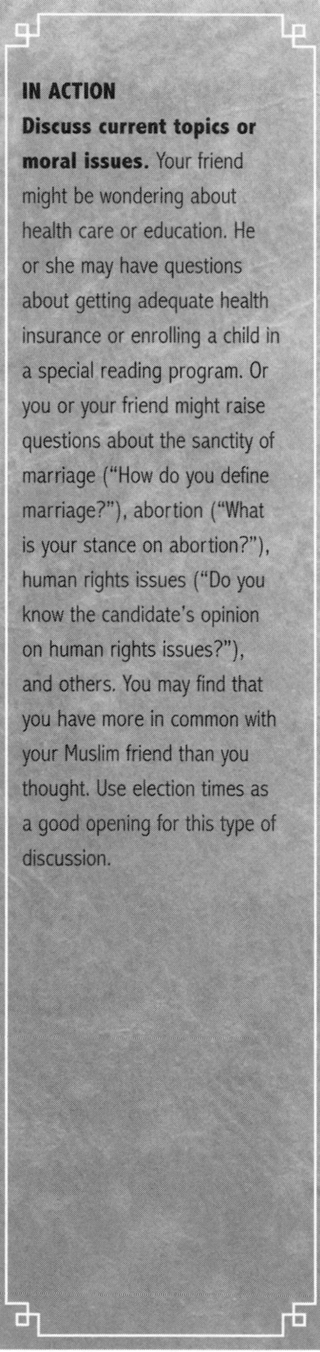

IN ACTION
Discuss current topics or moral issues. Your friend might be wondering about health care or education. He or she may have questions about getting adequate health insurance or enrolling a child in a special reading program. Or you or your friend might raise questions about the sanctity of marriage ("How do you define marriage?"), abortion ("What is your stance on abortion?"), human rights issues ("Do you know the candidate's opinion on human rights issues?"), and others. You may find that you have more in common with your Muslim friend than you thought. Use election times as a good opening for this type of discussion.

gives light as an act of gracious love. And if He is to be a just Judge, He must preserve His Word accurately so that we can be held accountable to it. If He were to allow it to be changed, then how could we know right from wrong and be held accountable?

We also understand that the "many versions" are merely translations with the same message. Interested individuals may learn Koine Greek and study the *Injeel* in the original language. Doing so shows that the original manuscripts contain one message, not a series of self-contradictory messages.

Your approach. It is important to follow a specific procedure when we talk to Muslims. A Muslim might say to you, "Isn't the *Injeel* corrupted?" Whenever they ask you this question, you need to respond on three levels: *theological*, *logical*, and *historical*.

1. *Theological reasoning*. Always start with the *theological*. Let's say you're sitting together over a cup of tea, and your friend says, "Well, the *Injeel* has been corrupted."

When Muslims say this or something like it, respond with "*Astaghfurullah!*" This Arabic expression means "God forbid" or "God forgive you for blasphemy." But you can use the English phrase, "God forbid." For example, you might say, in a loving, friendly way, "God forbid! I thought you believed in God." Of course your friend believes in God, but you're about to point out an inconsistency in their thinking.

Next read or recite an appropriate verse from the Bible, which is the Word of God and is able to answer for itself. I recommend Mark 13:31: "Heaven and earth will pass away, but my words will never pass away." Explain to your friend that if God sent the *Injeel*, God will protect it. No one is stronger than God, and no one can change His message if He chooses to keep it unchanged. Quran 2:148 is a beautiful verse that says, in essence, "God can do all things," and agrees with our Bible (for example, Luke 1:37; 18:27; Genesis 18:14).

Your friend would never deny that God is stronger than humans, but you need to help him or her see that one of the implications of God's power is that He can and does protect His Word.

You may recall the story in Chapter 3 of my phone conversation with the Sudanese woman who worked for the long distance company. She agreed to accept and read the *Injeel*, and I FedEx'd her one.

After that I prayed, *Lord, let that company call me again.* They called me again. The second time it was a Pakistani man. I shared my testimony with him, and he gave me his e-mail, so that I could follow up with him.

The third person to call me was an Iraqi man. I engaged him in conversation and offered to send him a copy of the *Injeel*.

His immediate response was, "It's corrupted. The *Injeel* has been changed."

The Truth is from thy Lord;
So be not at all in doubt....
For God
Hath power over all things.
—Quran 2:147-148

What is impossible with men
is possible with God.
—Jesus in Luke 18:27

RESOURCES FOR YOU

Give a Bible. At ***crescentproject.org***, we've made available the Injeel (New Testament) in several of the most common languages of Muslims, including Arabic. Please visit our site for a gift that can change your Muslim friend's life and eternal destiny. Most Muslims will gladly accept a copy of the *Injeel*, especially if you present it privately, when no other Muslims are watching.

So I said to him in Arabic, "*Astaghfurullah!*"

"Why are you saying that?" he asked.

"You just insulted God."

"What do you mean?"

"You just told me that Christians or some other humans are stronger than God—that we can change the *Injeel* and that God cannot protect His Word from us."

As followers of Jesus, we take offense when people offend God. When people say that God's Word has been corrupted, they're saying that people are stronger than God, and that is impossible. Such a claim is offensive. We believe that there is no one stronger than God.

2. Logical reasoning. Now, at this point in your discussion with your friend, it's time to consider the *logical* approach to the integrity of the Bible. If your friend claims that the *Injeel* has been corrupted, he or she needs to deal with the following questions:

- Who changed the *Injeel*?
  Many will answer that the apostle Paul was the primary culprit. In any case, they will typically claim that Christians made the changes, devising numerous versions of the Bible over the years.
- Why would somebody want to change the *Injeel*?
  This one is harder to answer, but the most common response is that the changes were motivated by the Christians' unwillingness to have faith in the true God, Allah, or His prophet, Muhammad.
- Where was the *Injeel* corrupted?
  This answer may vary, but many believe that Paul or other Christians made the changes at Rome.
- Where is the original *Injeel*?
  This question is also difficult for Muslims to answer. If anyone could find the original, unchanged *Injeel*, then they could prove to the world what God genuinely taught through Jesus. Since no such "uncorrupted" *Injeel* has ever been found in all these centuries, the only conclusion is that it has been destroyed or lost. Or that it never existed, and the *Injeel* was never changed.

- What parts of the *Injeel* are corrupted?
  The standard answer is that Christians changed many stories and deleted all mentions of Islam and Muhammad. However, there is no research to back up this claim. If it were true, archeologists should have discovered evidence of the in-between versions of the *Injeel*—between the "original" and the Bible we have today. Not a single sign of these versions exists in any manuscripts or other historical documents.

  What confuses many Muslims is the existence of so many versions or translations of the Bible today. You can explain that these are simply different translations from the same manuscripts. The original-language, Greek and Hebrew Bible is one message, and translators have chosen words in English and other modern languages to convey that one message.
- When was the *Injeel* corrupted? Was it before or after the life of Muhammad?
  This final question is very important, so we'll give it special attention. Some claim that Paul changed the *Injeel* in AD 325. But since Paul died around AD 63-64—more than 260 years earlier—this is impossible.

Muhammad, on the other hand, lived AD 570-632, and he announced that he was a prophet in 610. If the *Injeel* had been corrupted before Muhammad's time, then Christians would have been following a corrupt book for hundreds of years, and Muhammad would have warned his followers away from the "corrupted" *Injeel*. But, in fact, the Quran states clearly that it came to *confirm*—not to replace or correct—the message of Jesus, and that Muhammad instructed his followers to believe in the *Tawrat* of Moses, the *Zabur* of David, and the *Injeel* of Jesus (Quran 3:2-3).

The bottom line is that not once does the Quran say that any of the portions of our Bible have been changed. This assertion has been added by men. When you invite a Muslim to read the Bible, you are not asking them to do anything wrong. In fact, you're asking them to obey the teaching of the Quran and follow the teachings of Jesus.

Whether one believes the Bible was corrupted before or after Muhammad, the majority of Muslims will tell you, "We don't know the answer." In fact, the folk Islam taught by the *imams* has no satisfying answers to any of our questions. So we need to help our Muslim friend take a closer look at the history of the *Injeel*.

3. *Historical reasoning*. After you've explained to your friend the theological and logical reasoning, it's time to look into the *historical* approach to the *Injeel's* integrity. Here's a simple way to use a diagram and a few historical facts to prove that the *Injeel* has never been changed.

Start by drawing a long horizontal line, then divide it into three segments, as shown below.

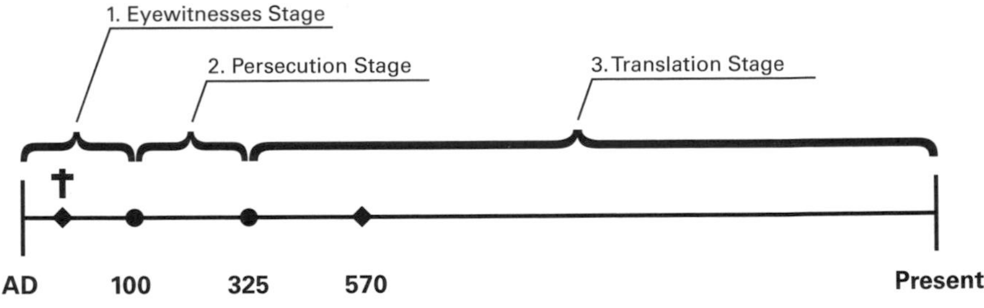

Then explain these three time periods to your Muslim friend. Segment A, the Eyewitness Stage (AD 1-100), is the period during which lived the eyewitnesses of Jesus' life, miracles, teachings, crucifixion, and resurrection. During this time the *Injeel* couldn't have been changed, because those who knew the truth firsthand would have stood up and confronted the lie. They saw Him heal the sick, raise the dead, feed the five thousand, cast out demons, and walk across the Sea of Galilee. They knew that Jesus genuinely died on the cross, that He was buried, and that He rose from the dead. They knew that Jesus' tomb was empty, that no one hid His body, that He appeared in a glorified body, and that He ascended into heaven.

But what if the eyewitnesses were the liars? you might ask. *What if they were the ones who changed the* Injeel*?* Good question. Hundreds of eyewitnesses of Jesus' life were martyred for their Christian faith, including the apostle Peter and ten more of Jesus' twelve disciples, and later the apostle

Paul. In other words, if they changed the *Injeel*, then they were willing to die for a lie they fabricated. People don't do that. People will only be martyred for the truth. And so during the Eyewitness Stage the *Injeel* could not have been changed.

After AD 100, the eyewitnesses of Jesus' life were all gone. This begins Segment B, the Persecution Stage (AD 100-325). Throughout this period we find frequent persecution of the Christians. They were killed and their Scripture manuscripts were burned. However, from throughout the Mediterranean world we have found thousands of manuscripts from that period. No one of these manuscript contains the entire New Testament, but taken together the whole body of manuscripts contains the whole New Testament.

What is more, the church fathers—the generations of church leaders who continued on after the original disciples had died—wrote numerous letters, sermons, and other documents that included Bible quotations.

All of these manuscripts, fragments, letters, and other documents that contain portions of the New Testament are in Greek. If the *Injeel* was changed during this period of time, we would expect numerous contradictions between the thousands of different documents, reflecting the older and newer (changed) versions. But guess what. All of these documents agree with each other.

CHAMPION FOR CHRIST

Maintain a consistent lifestyle. Live so that your friend can see the difference between you and the culture around you. The Gospel of Christ is the power of God for salvation from sin and deliverance from sin's power.

When you compare passages from one source to another, with only insignificant grammatical variations, they're all the same. Our conclusion: The *Injeel* was not changed during this time period.

Now when we come to Segment C, the Translation Stage (AD 325 to present), in which we live today, we begin finding complete copies of the Greek New Testament. The oldest copy of the entire New Testament is Codex Sinaiticus, which dates back to AD 325. Two others are Codex Vaticanus, dated AD 350, and Codex Alexandrinus, dated AD 400. These agree with each other and with the Persecution Stage manuscript evidence. In other words, the *Injeel* in Segments B and C is the same; it was not changed.

What about all the present-day translations? These are all translated directly from the Greek manuscripts, the most reliable of which are dated between AD 100 and 400. Today's translations contain exactly the same message and meaning as in the Greek manuscripts—just in a different language. The *Injeel* of AD 325 is the same as the *Injeel* of today; it has not been changed.

In all three historical stages from Jesus to today, the *Injeel* contains the verse where Jesus said, "I am the way, the truth, and the life," among hundreds of other uniquely Christian truth claims. If Jesus had said, "Muhammad is coming after Me," someone would have written it down during the Eyewitness Stage, it would show up in the manuscripts of the Persecution Stage and the Translation Stage, and it would be in our translations today. If Jesus had said, "I'm only one of many ways," we would see it copied over and over among the thousands of Greek manuscripts, and someone would include it a modern translation somewhere today. But no such statements exist anywhere in the chain of the *Injeel's* existence. It is consistent. The message that Jesus taught is the same as the message of our New Testament translations today.

The Point of Decision

Once your Muslim friend recognizes the truth of the *Injeel's* integrity, what is next? Theologically, it's inescapable that God is strong enough to protect and keep His message, which He sent to enlighten us. Logically, the only satisfying answers to the key questions is that the New Testament has not been changed. And historically, all the evidence indicates that our Bible is the same as the original message God sent. Your friend might even be eager to read the *Injeel* and respect it as God's message. This is tremendous progress, but the bridge is not yet complete.

Your friend may have had a change of mind, but has he experienced a change of will? When you ask, "Would you like to receive Jesus as your Savior?" does she say yes? The bridge is complete when you've reached the point of decision. If God sent the *Injeel* and if God has exerted His almighty power to preserve it, He did so to teach us about redemption and to bring us to salvation in Jesus. Encourage your Muslim friend to take Jesus as his Lord and Savior. Use this bridge to explain why Jesus is the only way. Because the *Injeel* says that He is the only way.

Don't be pushy. Be patient. This is often new information, and your friend is considering a radical change in his or her entire view of reality and eternity. Think of this opportunity as a spiritual thermometer, to measure the spiritual temperature of your Muslim friend—their readiness for the good news. If they're not ready, you may want to explore and find out what issues are holding them back from repenting and accepting Christ as Savior.

Your friend is likely to say something like, "I'm sorry, this is all new for me." Accept his reluctance graciously; it's normal. Simply ask, "Would you like to read the *Injeel*?" Most Muslims, after they've heard the theological, logical, and historical reasoning above, will gladly accept a copy. Give your friend time. He might want to study the Bible with you.

In some conversations, you might be able to talk through all three part of the approach we've outlined. Sometimes you might be wise to focus only on one or two components. You might adequately cover, say, the logical reasoning in one conversation, or you might need to come back to it several times over a period of days or weeks.

Don't overstay your welcome in any one conversation, but keep building your friendship, and keep coming patiently back to your friend with love and truth. Keep gently affirming the same simple truths, starting with facts that your friend already believes and working across the bridge to new truth.

Most of your time with your friend you will spend explaining and repeating. That's good. Just keep your focus always on Jesus Christ and the unchanging New Testament. The time will be well spent. When you've answered the question, Is the *Injeel* corrupted? you've answered the most common question for Muslims. You've brought them to the heart of the gospel—that Jesus lived, was crucified, and rose from the dead. You've helped your friend accept the basis for all the most important truths about life and eternity—the way of salvation and the way to live a fulfilling life, pleasing to God.

When you've answered the question, Is the *Injeel* corrupted? you've answered the most common question for Muslims.

In Attitude

Our heavenly Father, thank you for protecting Your written message to us. Thank You that You are more powerful than anyone. Thank You for providing in the Bible everything we need for faith, life, and Christlike conduct. Give me the wisdom to study it and the strength to obey it. I ask this for the sake of Jesus.

Chapter Ten

Building a Bridge to Salvation

At a national chain book store, I met Muhammad from Pakistan, and we started to discuss religion and culture. "My Pakistani friend," I asked, "how do people go to heaven?"

"By good works," he answered. "Life is a test, and on Judgment Day God will weigh my good and bad works on the scale. I can show God that I've done more good than bad. Even if it's 51 percent good, I'll go heaven."

Then I asked, "What if a person's works end up weighing fifty-fifty, half good and half bad? Where would that person go?"

He stared at me for a moment, then answered, "I'm not sure. But my name is Muhammad. I'm sure God will not let me stay in hell too long."

When a man tells you that his salvation hangs on his sharing a name with a prophet, then you know that Islam does not have a satisfying answer to the problem of sin.

Enslaved by the Scales: The Problem of Sin in Islam

There is one Christian belief with which no Muslim will argue—namely, that man is sinful. The Quran teaches that all humans (except Jesus) have sinned. In fact, twice the Quran mentions that God forgave Muhammad for his sins. (Quran 47:19; 48:1). The *imams* teach that the prophets were all sinless, but that is not what the Quran says.

Christianity and Islam agree that everyone (except Jesus) has committed sins and that our sins require a price to be paid. Muslims do not believe in original sin. *Why should I be accountable for what Adam did?* they

The child is born sinless, he has no sins. As he grows up, he puts on the extra baggage. Some people put on more, some people less.
—A Muslim man

IN ACTION [FOR WOMEN]

Join a gym exclusively for women. Your friends may be more comfortable working out in a ladies-only gym. Schedule "tea time" after workouts for further interaction.

Provide an environment to be in the sun. When Muslim women cover, sometimes they are unable to get enough Vitamin D from sun exposure, which has resulted in outbreaks of rickets. This can be solved by simply spending time outdoors on sunny days. Try walking, playing tennis, taking the kids to the neighborhood pool, or participating in other outdoor leisure activities.

reason. They believe each person is born like a blank page and commits sins that are written to his account. But we don't need to dwell on our differences; rather, we should build bridges by highlighting our similarities. It's enough that we agree that all of us have sinned and have a problem that needs solving.

Not only do we agree on the sinfulness of humanity, but both the Bible and the Quran teach that Jesus was the only pure, sinless human ever born. Even among the prophets, He was the only sinless prophet (Quran 19:19, 34-35, 3:53-60). This is very important and will come into play in our approach to the question of salvation.

Now we come to a major difference between Islam and Christianity. Sin is the problem. We agree. But what to do about sin? The Bible teaches that we cannot earn our salvation; it is purely by grace—a free gift from God, paid for by the sacrifice of Jesus on the cross. The Quran, however, teaches that one can only enter Paradise by doing enough good works to balance and erase his bad works. And even then, salvation is never certain.

The Muslim's logic. Whenever Muslims hear us talk about salvation by grace, they say, "We take responsibility for our sins, while you Christians sin as much as you want and stick your sins to Jesus." They believe that Christians are lazy and morally loose, because we don't try to erase our sins with good works; that we keep on sinning and Jesus keeps on forgiving. To them, this is illogical. It makes sense, rather, that each individual should pay the price (in good works or in punishment) for his own sin. "Why should Jesus die for anyone else?" they reason. "It's not fair that Christ should pay for my sins. Everyone should pay for his own sins."

What is more, Muslims have a serious problem with the cross of Christ. In their thinking, an almighty God and His righteous prophets must always triumph; to admit that Jesus was crucified is to admit defeat and to cast disrespect on both God and His prophet, Jesus. God can never lose; He always wins.

Rather, most Muslims believe that Jesus did not die on the cross, and that the Romans and Jews did not thereby win over Him. Muslims choose to interpret one or two verses from the Quran to mean that Jesus was lifted up to heaven and did not die.

And why would anyone need a sacrifice for their sins anyway? Muslims pride themselves in being able to do good works to balance out and erase their bad works, thereby obtaining righteousness in God's sight. After all, Quran 7:7-9 tells about the Judgment Day, when our good works and our sins are weighed against each other in the balance. So no one has a need for Jesus to die in their place.

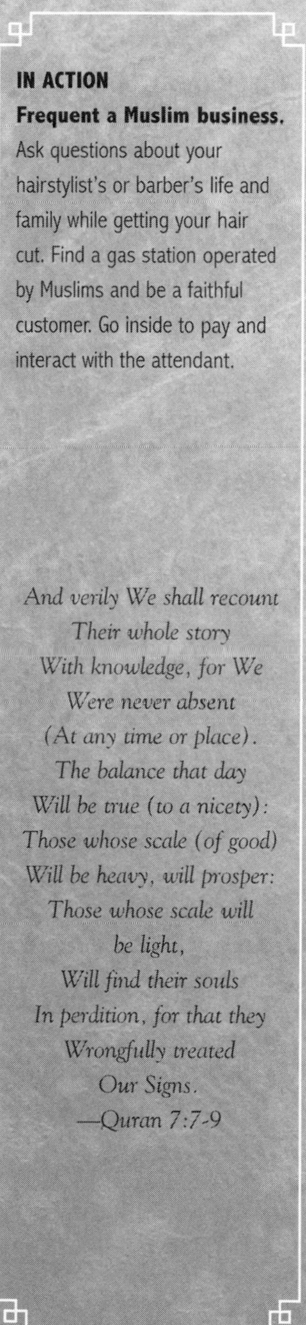

IN ACTION

Frequent a Muslim business. Ask questions about your hairstylist's or barber's life and family while getting your hair cut. Find a gas station operated by Muslims and be a faithful customer. Go inside to pay and interact with the attendant.

And verily We shall recount
Their whole story
With knowledge, for We
Were never absent
(At any time or place).
The balance that day
Will be true (to a nicety):
Those whose scale (of good)
Will be heavy, will prosper:
Those whose scale will
be light,
Will find their souls
In perdition, for that they
Wrongfully treated
Our Signs.
—Quran 7:7-9

Nobody knows that they will be able to get into paradise. Even Prophet Muhammad, peace be upon him, said, "My good work is not going to take me to paradise; God's mercy is going to take me to paradise." Everybody is waiting, is working, and waiting until Judgment Day comes, hoping for God's mercy.
—A Muslim man

IN ACTION [FOR FAMILIES]
Invite them to your child's birthday party. If your child has a Muslim classmate, invite them to a party. Call the parent and explain what will be happening at the event. Ask if he or she would like to be present and help with the setup.

Provide good, clean fun. Muslim parents can struggle with allowing their children to mix with non-Muslims, fearing they may be poorly influenced. Church youth group events, movie nights, and game nights can provide a safe environment for Muslim parents to send their kids.

The *imams* teach that God is a just judge, and He knows everything about your life. If you sin, you pay for your sin. If I sin, I pay for my sin. And God is a good businessman; no one can fool Him or steal from Him.

Muslims believe that life is a test and on Judgment Day your individual good works will save you, cover you sins, and get you into paradise.

Understanding Jesus' Sacrifice

So Islam and Christianity both agree that all humans (except Jesus) have a problem—sin. And that problem must be solved if we have any hope of spending eternity in heaven or paradise with God. Muslims know the guilt and experience the shame of sin. How do we Christians answer the problem of sin?

Biblical foundation. First, *we all have sinned.* We believe the Bible when it says that no one is righteous (see Romans 3:10-12, 23). The Bible teaches that God is holy, all of the time. Just as you cannot mix night and day, our holy God cannot mix with sin. All humans (except Jesus) have sinned, and it doesn't matter whether you've sinned a little bit or a lot—you've sinned. A bottle that is broken a little bit is still broken. A balloon that is pierced by a small pin is still popped. One sin makes a person less than perfect, less than holy. And only perfect holiness can mix with our holy God.

Second, *our good works are good, but they're are not enough.* The Bible teaches that no one is able to achieve his or her own righteousness through good works (see Galatians 2:16). James 2:10 says, "Whoever keeps the whole law and yet stumbles at just one point is guilty of breaking all of it." Jesus said, in the Sermon on the Mount, "If you look on a woman lustfully, it's like you've committed adultery with her. And if you hate your brother, it's like you've killed him" (my paraphrase; see Matthew 5:21-22, 27-28). You and I can try to pass the righteousness test; you and I can do good works, but no amount of good works are good enough. We can never pass the test because we have already failed it, all of us.

Third, *our sin demands a life sentence.* When you sin, you have insulted God. Romans 6:23 says, "The wages of sin is death." So, left on our own, all of us must pay with our death—that is, eternal separation from God.

Fourth, *we all need a savior who can pay our debt and carry our shame.* We're helpless to save ourselves. And so all of us need salvation through an eternal sacrifice. But who can be this sacrifice? Certainly not another sinner. No one who has his own debt is able to pay anyone else's debt; a sinner cannot redeem another sinner. Our savior would need to be sinless.

Fifth, *only sinless Jesus could be our Savior.* God's holiness demands that He

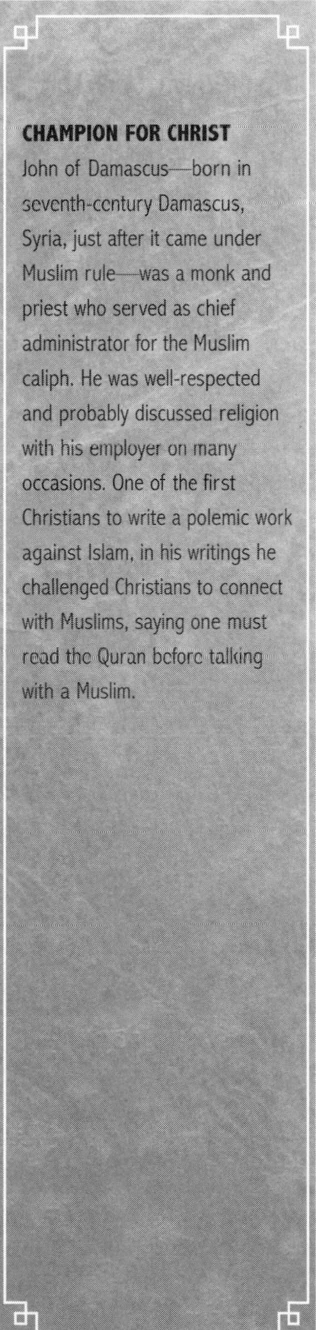

CHAMPION FOR CHRIST

John of Damascus—born in seventh-century Damascus, Syria, just after it came under Muslim rule—was a monk and priest who served as chief administrator for the Muslim caliph. He was well-respected and probably discussed religion with his employer on many occasions. One of the first Christians to write a polemic work against Islam, in his writings he challenged Christians to connect with Muslims, saying one must read the Quran before talking with a Muslim.

judges all of us, but amazingly God's love compelled Him to find a way out, and He found Jesus. "Salvation is found in no one else, for there is no other name under heaven given to men by which we must be saved" (Acts 4:12).

Sixth, *Jesus did not lose by dying on Friday; He won by conquering sin, Satan, and death on Sunday.* Jesus, the only sinless human, was the only one who could serve as a sacrificial Savior for other humans, to take their life sentence upon Himself. That's why we believe that the crucifixion and the resurrection were necessary for the salvation of humanity. In 2 Corinthians 5:21, the Bible says, "God made him who had no sin to be sin for us, so that in him we might become the righteousness of God." Elsewhere, the Bible says that we who receive Christ's sacrificial gift get to participate in His death (our debt is paid) and in His victorious resurrection (we receive eternal life; Philippians 3:10-11).

Seventh, *our salvation can only be by grace—God's free gift.* Our salvation cannot be earned by anything we do. It is a free gift from a loving God. The Bible uses the word "grace," which means gift (see Ephesians 2:8-9).

Finally, *we receive God's gift by faith.* God offers salvation freely, but for anyone to be saved he has to take a step of his own—faith. In other words, we receive salvation by trusting that God is faithful to keep His promise.

Over the centuries, there have been many good leaders, many good teachers, and many prophets that have come. But only sinless, sacrificial Jesus saves us from our sin.

How to Approach Your Muslim Friend

When you're in a conversation with a Muslim, you're almost certain to encounter the issue of how to solve the problem of sin. Maybe she says, "Jesus should not have died." Or he claims, "I'm saved by my good works." Where should you take the conversation next?

First, ask questions. That's the way to continue the conversation on the right foot. Asking friendly, thoughtful questions makes your friend think about his assumptions. It causes her to reason logically through territory she may never have explored before.

In this situation, I like to ask, "What happens on Judgment Day if God puts your good works and your bad works on the scale and they end up being perfectly equal—fifty-fifty? Where would you go then—to paradise or to hell?"

Most of your Muslim friends will be bewildered; they won't know what to answer. On the other hand, some might come back with a variety of responses, like, "My name is

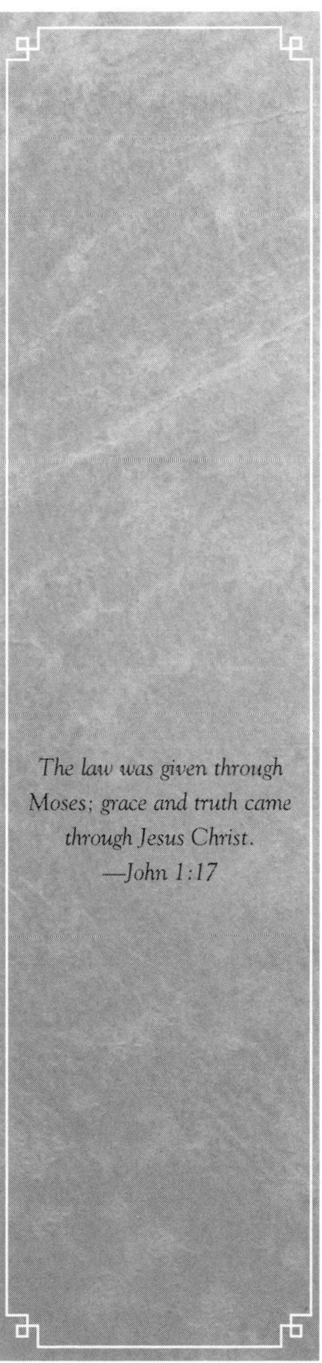

Muhammad, I'll only go to hell a little bit." Or, "I was born in Saudi Arabia, I'll just go to hell a little bit." I was refreshed by the honesty of one man who told me, "I hope the mercy of God will tip the scale toward the good." I like that! (I proceeded to show him that the mercy of God was Jesus, who tips the scale for us.)

Second, explain that all of us need a redeemer to save us from the penalty and power of sin. As we've seen, the penalty of sin is death or eternal separation from God; we need a redeemer to make possible our eternity in heaven. And the power of sin is to keep us sinning; we need a redeemer to change us inside, to give us a new character, to make it possible for us to choose not to sin.

Third, introduce your friend to the concept of grace, which literally means "gift." God offers salvation freely, because we are helpless to earn our own way to heaven.

Fourth, explain the following five points about God's character, each of which corresponds to one of the Islamic names of God.

1. God is Love (*Al Wadud*, "The Affectionate"). Muslims agree that God cares about His creation. What is more, the Bible says that He loves every human and wants to spend eternity with us (2 Peter 3:9).

2. God is Holy (*Al Qudoos*, "The Holy One"). The holiness of God demands that He separates Himself from sin.

3. God is Just (*Al Adil*, "The Just"). God must punish sin. The sinners are stuck to the sin, so they get punished with sin. Romans 6:23 says, "The wages of sin is death," or eternal separation from God.

4. God is Merciful (*Al Raheem*, "The Merciful"). God's mercy appeared in Jesus. He sent Jesus to be our eternal sacrifice. Jesus died on the cross for our sins and rose from the dead to prove that His sacrifice was accepted.

This is a good time to remind your friend of the story of Abraham and Isaac (Genesis 22). When Abraham prepared to sacrifice his son, God said, "Stop," and provided a sheep in his place. So every year, seventy days after the end of Ramadan, Muslims kill a sheep to remember that God redeemed the son of Abraham with a sheep. I like to explain, "God's mercy was in Christ, who died as a lamb of God, as a redeemer to replace us. We were supposed to die; Christ died for us."

5. God is Forgiving (*Al Ghafoor*, "The Forgiver"). Why can we receive forgiveness? Because our sins have been taken by Jesus. First John 1:9 says, "If we confess our sins, he is faithful and just and will forgive us our sins and purify us from all unrighteousness." You and I can experience forgiveness now; we don't have to wait till Judgment Day. God promises that if we confess our sins, because of the work of Christ we can have forgiveness and eternal life.

Fifth, explain to your Muslim friend that Christ became our eternal sacrifice. Why Christ and no one else? Because...

1. Christ is unique in His birth. No one else was ever born of a virgin.

2. Christ is sinless. More specifically, He was sinless from birth, and the Quran agrees on that. He was pure. He could be the perfect sacrifice because He had no sin of His own to die for.

3. Christ performed miracles. He raised the dead, healed the sick, cast out demons, and commanded the weather, showing that He was uniquely endowed with God's authority. He was sent by God, *as* God, unlike any other person on earth.

4. Christ redeemed all who would accept His gift. Jesus said, "I lay down my life for my friends." Just as the Passover lamb died for the firstborn of Israel, just as the sheep died in the place of Abraham's son, so Christ died as a substitute or replacement for us. His act of redemption is at the heart of our faith.

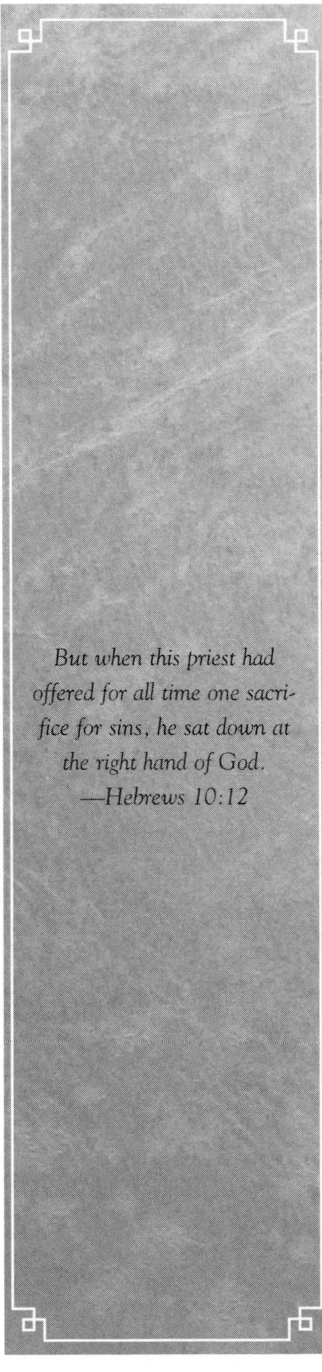

5. Christ rose from the dead. No prophet has risen from the dead except Jesus, the Christ, the Messiah. His resurrection proved that God accepted His sacrifice, that He is special, that He has power over sin, power over Satan, power over death.

6. Christ became the true *Adha*, the true Passover, the true sacrifice for us. Muslims understand the *Adha* sacrifice, celebrated seventy days after the end of Ramadan. Jesus became our eternal *Adha*. When you come to God and say, "Forgive me for my sins," because of what Jesus has done, God will forgive you. Someone paid your debt, someone died for your sins.

I have a friend from Saudi Arabia, named Ibrahim. Ibrahim and I became good friends, and he loves to go to Daytona Beach for spring break. He says he goes to swim, but given the reputation of that beach for its spring break activities, I suspect he has other motives. One day I said to Ibrahim, "Let's suppose you asked me to house sit, and while you were traveling I burnt the couch and I busted the television set. But before you returned, to 'pay' for your loss I vacuumed the apartment and washed your car." He smiled, and I continued. "When you come home, what would you think if I said to you, 'Ibrahim, forgive me for burning the couch and destroying television because I vacuumed and I washed your car'?"

He smiled again and said, "That has nothing to do with it. I left you here to take care of the house."

So I said to Ibrahim, "Exactly! Our good works are not good enough to pay for our sins, because when you sin, you sin against God Almighty. When you do good works, they're earthly works. They have nothing to do with your sin. When we do good works for God, that is great! It is our responsibility to be obedient. But that's an entirely separate issue from what must be done about our sin."

Jesus paid for the sins of everyone, sat down at the right hand of God, and intercedes for us daily. We don't have to wait for Judgment Day to see the intercession of Jesus. He is our redeemer and He gives us power to live a holy life.

The Point of Decision

When we talk to Muslims, we can easily fall short of our real goal for them. We can be satisfied when they nod and agree mentally, forgetting that we need to ask them to make a confession of faith.

The Muslim ritual practice is filled with tangible objections and actions. Before you pray, you wash. When you pray, you stand, kneel, and bow. So it's good to present the point of decision in a tangible way. I start by asking my Muslim friend, "Would you like to pray and receive Jesus?" I explain that prayer is a conversation with God, and that you can speak with God anywhere, anytime. The whole earth is a temple for Him.

Then I explain, "Your prayer must be divided into two parts: *Toub* and *Ish-had*. *Toub* means to repent or turn around. It implies you've been going one direction, but God wants you to turn around and go the other direction. You were going in the direction of disobedience and self-righteousness, trying to do good works to erase bad works. So *Toub*, repent, turn and go the other way.

"*Ish-had* means to confess or testify. Confess that Jesus is your only Savior from the penalty and power of sin. Testify that Jesus is your Redeemer."

This two-part approach to the decision provides a tangible,

understandable way for your Muslim friend to make a confession of faith to follow Christ. It's important to help your friend make that decision. Explain that he or she might do it alone at home, in a park, or in a car. That's fine. Or he or she might want to pray with you. What's important is that they respond genuinely to God's work in their heart.

Remember, this decision is the responsibility of God and your friend. Your job is not to make their decision for them; your job is to show them that Christ is the eternal sacrifice, and explain that they can repent and confess Him as their only Savior and their only Lord.

In Attitude

Our heavenly Father, thank You for giving me the great gift of salvation, paid for by the death of Your Son, Jesus. Grant me compassion for those who are living without You, and grant me wisdom to know how to talk with them about Your salvation. Help me to be Your faithful messenger, and to trust You to change the hearts of those who hear Your message. I ask this for the sake of Jesus.

Chapter Eleven

We're All God's Starters

When I came as an international student to America, I wanted to learn American culture, and my roommate taught me American football. He said, "Eleven players from each team play on the field."

My next question was, "Hey, what about the other players on the sidelines?"

He said, "Only the starters are on the field right now. The second- and third-string players are on the sidelines, waiting for the coach to put them in the game."

We are all on Jesus' team, but on Jesus' team there's no second string. We're all starters, and Jesus wants us all on the field. Today, 1.2 billion Muslims have never heard the words of Jesus. Seven million of them have moved to America and are still waiting for an authentic Christian witness. Our Lord Jesus said, "And this gospel of the kingdom will be preached in the whole world as a testimony to all nations, and then the end will come" (Matthew 24:14). In the last ten years more Muslims have become followers of Jesus than the previous fourteen hundred years. Why? Because Christians took the time to be friends with them, because Christians took the time to build bridges with them.

Jesus was very familiar with the agrarian society around Him, and He often used it to teach lessons about His kingdom. "The harvest is plentiful," He once said, "*but the workers are few.* Ask the Lord of the harvest, therefore, to send out workers into his harvest field" (Matthew 9:37-38, emphasis added).

I'll admit, I don't know much about farming. But I do live in Indiana and I have seen combines—huge, monstrous combines! Sometimes I drive through the Indiana countryside, gaping at these massive machines charging through fields. What I do know is that these machines are harvesting what was planted, and without them, the crops would be lost.

Can you imagine a harvest without harvesters? Jesus had one specific prayer request recorded in Matthew 9: He asked for workers for the harvest. If you will simply take what you've learned and walk willingly, availably into the field, God will sometimes assign you the task of harvester, and you'll enjoy the privilege of leading someone to salvation.

And just as the crops require harvesters, there would be nothing to harvest if it weren't for the planters. In some of your relationships, you may not see the end of the process—the unbeliever's step into belief, from darkness into light. But God might assign you the equally important task of planter, dissolving misconceptions, dismantling walls, telling truth, living love. Your patient, compassionate investment in the lives of Muslims will prepare their hearts for someone, in God's timing, to help those dear souls find their way to Jesus.

Today, Muslims are seeking to know and follow God. They desire fellowship with God, something made possible only through His mighty Word—Jesus Christ. Continue building friendships with Muslims. Continue sharing with them the great hope we have in Jesus.

Trust God. He is with you.

Get in the game.

"Even now the reaper draws his wages, even now he harvests the crop for eternal life, so that the sower and the reaper may be glad together. Thus the saying 'One sows and another reaps' is true."

—Jesus in John 4:36-37

In Attitude

Our heavenly Father, I pray that I will see that the harvest is white. Thank You for raising planters and harvesters. May I always serve You with joy whether I am sowing, watering, or reaping. May all glory go to You as I share the hope with Muslims for the sake of Jesus. Amen

Endnotes

1. For example, see FreeQuran.com.
2. Accessed 5/13/09 http://en.wikipedia.org/wiki/Qur%27an_desecration_controversy_of_2005.
3. NYTimes.com article http://www.nytimes.com/2008/12/23/us/23muslim.html?_r=2&ref=us
4. Accessed 6/8/2007 http://news.bbc.co.uk/2/hi/asia-pacific/6703155.stm
5. Accessed 5/11/09 http://www.nytimes.com/2007/05/30/world/asia/30cnd-malaysia.html?_r=1&scp=3&sq=lina%20joy&st=cse
6. Accessed 5/13/09 www.npr.org/templates/story/story.php?storyId=100961321
7. Accessed 9/4/11 http://articles.nydailynews.com/2011-03-09/news/28689293_1_muzzammil-hassan-aasiya-hassan-beheading
8. "Why Muslims Follow Jesus," *Christianity Today*. Accessed 5/20/09 http://www.christianitytoday.com/ct/2007/october/42.80.html?start=4
9. Pink Floyd, *Comfortably Numb 1979*

Appendix A

Jesus in the Qur'an and the *Injeel*

TITLES	QUR'AN	BIBLE
Word of God. His (God's) Word (Klimat Allah)	3:34,39,40,45; 4:169,171	John 1:1,14
A Word of Truth (Qawl Al-haqq)	19:34,35	John 4:6; Ephesians 1:13
The Truth from your Lord (Al-haqq)	3:53,60	John 8:32-36; 14:6
A Spirit of God (Ruh)	4:169,171; 17; 21:91	Matthew 12:28; Luke 1:35
The Messiah (Al-Masih)	3:40,45; 4:156,157	Matthew 16:16; John 1:41
Apostle [Messenger] (Rasul)	2:81,87; 254, 253; 3:43,49	Hebrews 3:1; Matthew 10:40
Prophet (Nabiyy)	2:130,136; 4:161,163	Matthew 21:11; Luke 4:24
Servant of God	4:170,172; 19:31	Matthew 12:18; John 4:34
Son of Mary (Ibn Maryam)	40, 45; 4:157; 171	Luke 2:48
Witness on Resurrection Day (Shahid)	4:45,41,157,159; 5:117	Matthew 24
Witness of [over] the people	3:120,117	John 5:30
Mercy from God (Rahmah)	19:21	Matthew 9:27-30
Bearer of Wisdom (Hikmah)	43:63	Luke 2:40,52
Knowledge of the Hour ('Ilm)	43:61	Matthew 24:36-44; John 4:25
Sign to all beings (Ayah)	3:44,50; 19:21; 21:91	Matthew 2:2-29
An Example [Pattern] (Mathal)	43:57,59	John 13:1-11

TITLES	QUR'AN	BIBLE
The Miracle Worker	3:49	Mark 1:34; 5:41,42; 6:33
Revelation to Mankind (Ayah)	19:21	Luke 2:10,30-32
The one to be followed	43:61	John 1:37; John 10:27
The one to be obeyed	3:44,50	Matthew 17:5; 8:27; Mark 1:3
Giver [Bringer] of Good Tidings	61:6	Luke 4:18; Acts 10:38
One of the Righteous (min Salihin)	3:40,46	Matthew 27:19; 2 Timothy 4
Knowledgeable in Scriptures	3:43,48; 5:109,110	Matthew 12:25; John 4:25
Like Adam (Mathal al Adama)	3:52,59	1 Corinthians 15:45-47
The Faultless [Holy, Most Pure]	19:19	Luke 23:4,14,41; Acts 2:14
One of the Closest to God (Min al Muquarrabin)	3:40,41; 7:111,114	John 14:9,10; Hebrews 2:9
High-honored [Eminent] in this world and Hereafter (Wajih)	3:40,45	Philippians 2:9,10
The Blessed One (Mubarak)	19:32,31	Matthew 21:9 Luke 1:42
The Favored One	43:59	John 1:18; Mark 1:11
The One Confirmed [Strengthened] with the Holy Spirit (Ruh-Al-Quds)	2:81,87,254,253	Mark 1:11; Luke 4:14
The Noble; Lordly (Sayyid)	3:39	Matthew 21:8-10
The Chaste	3:39	2 Corinthians 5:21; 1 Peter 2:21

TITLES	QUR'AN	BIBLE
Man of Peace (Salam)	19:34,33	Isaiah 9:6; Daniel 19:25
A Perfect Man (Sawiy)	19:17	1 Corinthians 13:10
The Conquerer (Al Ghaleb)		Revelation 19:11, 15
King of Kings		Revelation 19:16
Resurrection	19:15; 3:55; 4:158	Matthew 26—28 Mark 15—16 Luke 22—24 John 18—21

Notes

Notes

Notes

Notes

How can
YOU
reach her?
BRIDGES
Christians Connecting with Muslims
A small-group study by Crescent Project that demystifies Islam and empowers Christians to share the Gospel with Muslims
www.bridgesstudy.com
crescent project
HOPE WORTH SHARING
LifeWay

Adha
in the
Injeel
Fuad Issa